Sugar Butter Flour

THE WAITRESS PIE BOOK

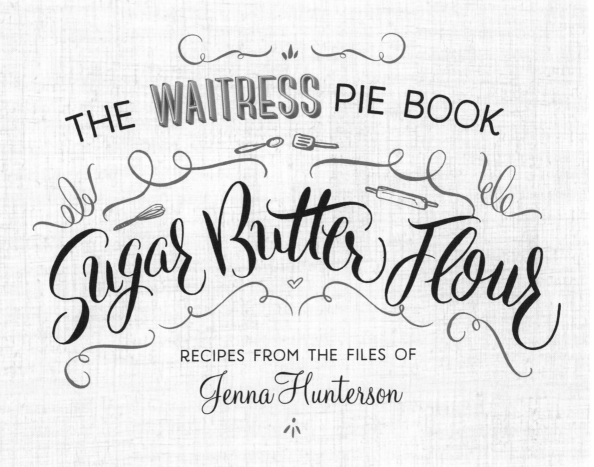

Sugar Butter Flour

RECIPES FROM THE FILES OF
Jenna Hunterson

TEXT BY DANIEL GERCKE · RECIPES BY SHERI CASTLE

PHOTOGRAPHS BY EVAN SUNG

PAM KRAUSS BOOKS/AVERY

NEW YORK

Pam Krauss Books / Avery
an imprint of Penguin Random House LLC
375 Hudson Street
New York, New York 10014

Most Avery books are available at special quantity discounts
for bulk purchase for sales promotions, premiums,
fund-raising, and educational needs. Special books or
book excerpts also can be created to fit specific needs.
For details, write SpecialMarkets@penguinrandomhouse.com.

Library of Congress Cataloging-in-Publication Data

Names: Hunterson, Jenna, author. | Gercke, Daniel.
Title: Sugar, butter, flour : the waitress pie book / recipes from the files
   of Jenna Hunterson ; text by Daniel Gercke.
Description: New York : Pam Krauss/Avery, [2017] | Includes index.
Identifiers: LCCN 2016056955 | ISBN 9780735216334 (hardback)
Subjects: LCSH: Pies. |
BISAC: COOKING / Courses & Dishes / Pies. | COOKING / Methods / Baking. |
PERFORMING ARTS / Theater / Broadway & Musical Revue. | LCGFT:
Cookbooks.
Classification: LCC TX773 .H8427 2017 | DDC 641.86/52—dc23
LC record available at https://lccn.loc.gov/2016056955
p.   cm.

Printed in the United States of America
10 9 8 7 6 5 4 3

Book design by Ashley Tucker

Dedicated to the memory of
Adrienne Shelly, the writer, director,
and star of the 2007 film *Waitress*,
and the team who was inspired to
adapt her story into an original
Broadway musical led by bookwriter
Jessie Nelson, composer/lyricist
Sara Bareilles, choreographer Lorin
Latarro, and director Diane Paulus.

~

MAKE IT WORK

MAKE IT EASY

MAKE IT CLEVER

CRAFT IT INTO PIECES

MAKE IT SWEET

CRIMP THE EDGES

OR MAKE IT SOUR AND SERVE WITH LEMON WEDGES

EVEN DOUBT CAN BE DELICIOUS

AND IT WASHES OFF ALL THE DIRTY DISHES

WHEN IT'S DONE I CAN SMILE

IT'S ON SOMEONE ELSE'S PLATE FOR A WHILE

I'LL PLACE IT ON DISPLAY

AND THEN I'LL SLICE AND SERVE MY WORRIES AWAY

CAUSE I CAN FIX THIS

I CAN TWIST IT INTO

SUGAR BUTTER COVERED PIECES

NEVER MIND WHAT'S UNDERNEATH IT

I HAVE DONE IT BEFORE

I'LL BAKE ME A DOOR TO HELP ME GET THROUGH . . .

I LEARNED THAT FROM YOU

MAMA, IT'S AMAZING WHAT BAKING CAN DO

-"WHAT BAKING CAN DO," SARA BAREILLES

~

Contents

Introduction

My mama taught me everything I know about pies. It was in her kitchen that I learned that making a pie is an act of love, and how baking can open a door to a better life. Mama came up with hundreds of different pies and they all had real funny names, like Lonely Chicago Pie and Sweet Victory Pie. She told me, "Jenna, you can tell a whole story with a taste."

Well she was right. And now I share my story with you through the recipes in this book.

It's a story of how I lost my way, but ultimately dared to take a long forgotten dream off the shelf and trust that baking could open a door to a better life.

I learned that you don't bake a pie with your hands, you bake it with your heart. It requires the essential ingredients: a dash of hope, a cup of courage, a little spice, and some good friends to share it with in the end.

Oh, and don't forget sugar, butter, and flour.

Jenna's Rules for Baking (and Life)

There's not much to making a good pie. You can follow a recipe, or just follow your heart. And no matter how big the mess, you can always start fresh. If only life were as easy as pie.

① KEEP COOL. Pastry dough is much easier to work with when it's chilled. If it warms up during handling, feel free to stick it back in the fridge to cool it down some. After you make your dough, shape it into a 6-inch disk and let it rest in the fridge overnight. The dough needs a good night's rest to relax the gluten, firm the butter, and prevent it from socking its damn fool husband in the nose during breakfast. And besides, it'll shrink less when you bake it.

② KEEP MOVING. When you roll out your crust, you want to keep it moving. Rotate the dough a quarter turn every couple of passes with the roller to stop it from sticking. Stay too long in one place, and you're going to stick to the counter—and trust me: it's real hard to get unstuck. That's how I got into this mess in the first place. Sure do wish I'd followed this rule before I went and got myself married.

③ VENT. When things get hot in the oven, there will be steam. Where's all that steam going to go? It's going to blow through your top crust, that's where. Right through any place you patched a hole or tried to cover up a mistake. So be sure to poke vents in your crust before baking, and make certain you got a couple of good friends around to talk out your troubles with. Because blowing your top is not going to help your pie one bit.

④ HOLD IT TOGETHER. It's hard to say for sure what pie is. There's some don't even have crusts. But if you look, every kind of pie's got something holding it together. Whether it's a crust, a ramekin, a jar, a few good friends, or just some crazy fantasies of owning their own pie shop someday, there's always something that embraces the pie and keeps it from falling apart. That's what pie really is—a bunch of wonderful things that go perfectly together and manage not to fall apart.

Pie Crusts: The Basics

People get all tangled up over pie crust, but like anything in life, it gets easier once you've done it a few times. There's really not much you can do to mess this up if you take it slow, follow the directions, and leave yourself enough time so the dough can rest before you roll it out. And remember, it's basically just sugar, butter, flour—and when have they ever let you down?

Classic Pie Crust Pastry

You can make dough one crust at a time, but even if you're making a single-crust pie, why not make enough for two and freeze half for another day? If you let the dough defrost in the fridge overnight, you can start the day with a fresh-made pie just like we always did at the diner. To make the dough in the food processor, see the directions on page 18.

single crust

1¼ cups unbleached all-purpose flour

1 tablespoon sugar

½ teaspoon kosher salt

8 tablespoons (1 stick) unsalted butter, cut into small cubes and chilled

3 to 4 tablespoons ice-cold water

double crust

2½ cups unbleached all-purpose flour

2 tablespoons sugar

1 teaspoon kosher salt

1 cup (2 sticks) unsalted butter, cut into small cubes and chilled

6 to 8 tablespoons ice-cold water

to make the dough by hand

1. Whisk together the flour, sugar, and salt in a large bowl. Use two butter knives or a pastry blender to work in the butter until the mixture resembles coarse sand with about a third of the pieces of butter left the size of green peas. Sprinkle 3 tablespoons of the water over the flour mixture if making a single crust, 6 tablespoons for a double batch. Use a fork to toss the dry ingredients and fold in the water until the mixture forms clumps of shaggy dough. Pinch one of the clumps; if it holds together, it's ready; if it breaks apart easily, stir in more water, 1 teaspoon at a time. Use your fingertips (palms are too warm!) to gather the clumps into a ball. Divide the mass of dough in two if making a double batch.

2. Place each dough ball on a sheet of plastic wrap, flatten into a disk about ¾ inch thick, and wrap tightly. Refrigerate for at least 3 hours and up to 3 days. This gives the pastry time to rest, so the flour can continue to absorb the liquid and the pastry will be easier to handle. For longer storage, place the wrapped pastry in a freezer bag and freeze for up to 2 months. Thaw in the refrigerator overnight before using.

recipe continues

to make the dough in a food processor

1. Place the flour, sugar, and salt in the bowl of a food processor and pulse 4 or 5 times to combine. Scatter the pieces of butter over the flour mixture and pulse about 8 times or until the mixture resembles coarse sand with about a third of the pieces of butter left the size of green peas.

2. Remove the lid and sprinkle 3 table-spoons of the water over the flour mixture if making a single crust, 6 tablespoons for a double batch. Pulse about 6 times or until the mixture forms clumps of shaggy dough. Remove the lid and pinch one of the clumps; if it holds together, it's ready; if it breaks apart easily, add more water, 1 teaspoon at a time, and pulse to combine. Pour the clumps onto a work surface and use your fingertips (palms are too warm!) to gather the clumps into a ball. Divide the mass of dough in two if making a double batch.

3. Place each dough ball on a sheet of plastic wrap, flatten into a disk about ¾ inch thick, and wrap tightly. Refrigerate for at least 3 hours and up to 3 days. This gives the pastry time to rest, so the flour can continue to absorb the liquid and the pastry will be easier to handle. For longer storage, place the wrapped pastry in a freezer bag and freeze for up to 2 months. Thaw in the refrigerator overnight before using.

rolling and shaping your crust

1. Roll a disk of dough on a lightly floured surface into a round that is about 3 inches wider than the diameter of your pie pan. (If the chilled dough is so firm that it cracks when you try to roll it, let stand at room temperature for a few minutes, but not so long that the butter or other fats begin to melt.) Rotate the dough a quarter turn between rolls to help keep it round. Use enough flour to keep the pastry moving easily without sticking, but add no more than necessary because excess flour makes the pastry tough. Brush away any visible flour with a dry pastry brush.

2. Fit the round into a 9½-inch pie pan. There should be about ½ inch of overhang. Press together any holes or tears with a dampened fingertip. Fold under the edge of the pastry and crimp as desired. Refrigerate until deeply chilled, at least 1 hour, which helps the pie shell stay in place in the pan instead of scooting or slipping down, and also improves the texture of the pastry. Cold fat going into a hot oven is what makes the pastry flaky.

Blind Baking

For some recipes, the pie shells need to be partially or fully baked before they are filled. This process is called blind baking. A wet filling that cooks in the oven should go into a partially baked shell so the filling's moisture won't make the bottom soggy. A filling that is cooked ahead should go into a fully baked pie shell.

Dough for a single-crust classic pie shell (page 17)

for a partially blind-baked pie shell

1. Preheat the oven to 350°F. Roll out the dough to fit into your pie pan, transfer to the pan, and press gently into the corners. Line the dough with aluminum foil, making sure it covers the edge of the dough; use overlapping sheets if needed. Fill the foil to a depth of ½ inch with pie weights or dried beans. Place the pan on a rimmed baking sheet.

2. Bake in the upper third of the oven for 15 minutes, or until the crust is set and begins to dry but hasn't taken on any color. Fold up the corners of the foil and lift out the foil and weights. Bake for 10 minutes more, or until the shell is dry and pale golden. Place on a wire rack to cool to room temperature.

for a fully blind-baked pie shell

1. Preheat the oven to 350°F. Roll out the dough on a lightly floured surface to fit into your pie pan, transfer to the pan, and press gently into the corners. Line the dough with aluminum foil, making sure it covers the edge of the dough; use overlapping sheets if needed. Fill the foil with ½ inch of pie weights or dried beans. Place the pan on a rimmed baking sheet.

2. Bake in the upper third of the oven for 15 minutes, or until the crust is set and begins to dry but hasn't taken on any color. Fold up the corners of the foil and lift out the foil and weights. Bake for 15 to 20 minutes more, or until the pie shell is golden brown all over. Place on a wire rack to cool to room temperature.

WEIGHTY MATTERS

Pie weights hold the pastry in place in the tin as it bakes, which prevents bubbles and bumps from forming in the empty shell and keeps the sides from slumping and sagging. Some bakers purchase reusable ceramic pie weights or a metal pie chain, but it is fine to use 1 to 1½ pounds dry, uncooked rice or dried beans. The rice or beans cannot be cooked and eaten after they are used as weights, but can be saved to reuse for baking future pie crusts for several months, or as long as they smell fresh.

Crumb Crusts

A nice crumb crust joins up perfectly with the silky smoothness of most chocolate fillings and, because they are pressed into the pan, not rolled out like pastry dough, they are less intimidating for many bakers. You can use just about any cookie, cracker, or ice-cream cone for a crumb crust, as long as it's crisp. Cream-filled sandwich cookies are not a great choice, as they get too mushy when you pulverize them, but scrape the cream off and the cookies themselves will do just fine. The proportion of crumbs to butter stays the same no matter what kind of crumbs you go with, and you can replace up to ¼ cup of the crumbs with finely chopped nuts, if you're in the mood. To make crumbs, pulse the cookies or crackers in the bowl of a food processor until finely ground. Another option is to put the cookies or crackers in a large zip-top bag, squeeze out the air, and crush them with a rolling pin or the bottom of a heavy pan. Make sure they're crushed evenly so your crumb crust holds together well. Then mix the crumbs with the melted butter, combine thoroughly, and use your fingers to press the crumbs first up the sides of your pan and then firmly onto the bottom. Bake or fill as directed.

A Few Final Thoughts

PANS VS. PLATES. If a recipe specifies a pie pan or tin, use a metal pan. If it calls for a pie plate, the recipe will work best in a glass or ceramic pan. For most pies, however, the type of pan is not a deal breaker and they can be used interchangeably.

SIZE MATTERS. Not all pie pans labeled "9½ inches" measure exactly 9½ inches; they can range from about 9¼ to 10¼ inches. For most recipes, you can use pans marked "9½" or "10 inches" with sides at least 1½ inches deep. When using a store-bought pie shell, always select those marked "deep-dish" or they won't hold all your filling.

PART ONE

Baked from the Heart: Fruit Pies

I CAN'T THINK OF A BETTER WAY TO CELEBRATE A SEASON THAN with a fresh-baked fruit pie. Look at any diner menu board and you'll see summer is all about pies made from fresh peaches and plums, sweet cherries, and berries, all bursting with juice. When fall comes around, so do crisp apples and pears. Wrap those bright flavors in a tender crust and you can taste the season on your tongue. But fruit pies aren't just for that part of the calendar. In winter and early spring when fresh fruit might be scarce, you can always fall back on well-stored apples or frozen summer fruits like peaches and cherries. These off-season pies are like time capsules from the warmer months. So the fruit might be seasonal, but fruit pies stay on the menu all year long.

Fruit pies are also some of the simplest pies to make—but they turn out the best if you follow a few guidelines. First, start with good fruit. Not just any fruit will do for pie. You'll know it's right when you have to hold yourself back from gobbling it all up before it goes in the filling. If you use frozen fruit, make sure it's not bland. You can fuss all you want with the sweeteners and flavorings, but if your fruit is weak, all you'll taste are sugar and spice. On the other hand, good fruit will shine through any little mistakes you might make. Because let's face it: nobody's perfect. The heart of a fruit pie is the fruit, and the rest just supports it.

Second, adjust the sugar according to the sweetness of the fruit. Usually, the juicier the fruit, the sweeter it is, but I always give it a taste just to make sure. When you've got a whole lot of fresh fruit, peel it, slice it, and freeze it for a rainy day. Measure out the amount you need for your recipe and label it with a little note so you don't forget it's for pie. Berries and sliced peaches work best here, but you can do the same with cherries, rhubarb, and other fruits. Of course, if you couldn't resist eating all the leftovers on the spot, you can pick up frozen fruit at the supermarket whenever you need it.

Last thing is, you have to let off a little steam. Most fruit pies use a simple flaky crust, either single or double. If you're using a double crust, make sure you make an escape hatch for the moisture that accumulates under the lid by venting the top crust. You can make tidy little slits in the center, or get more creative: use a small cookie cutter to cut out polka dots, hearts, or apple shapes. Or make a lattice, which looks like more work than it is (see page 31).

Some of these pies swap a top crust for a crumbly streusel layer, which adds a bit of crunch and makes the whole pie a little bit sweeter and richer thanks to all the extra sugar and butter you mix into it. Keep it in mind if you ever feel like changing up a recipe that calls for a double crust. If you substitute streusel, you'll want to take down the sugar in the filling just a touch to make sure it all comes balanced and not too sweet.

~

SWEET VICTORY PIE

*A beautiful and golden lattice crust
with plump red cherries peeking through.*

THE APPLE OF MY EYE RUM RAISIN HAND PIES

*Creamy inside with sharp bursts of
sweetness from the raisins and apples.*

LIFE'S JUST PEACHY-KEEN POLKA-DOT PEACH PIE

*Bursting with sugar and sunshine,
this peach pie is that kind of showstopper.*

BANISH THE GLUM PLUM GALETTES

*Little beauties baked with tart plums
and spiced with cardamom.*

BIG GUY STRAWBERRY PIE

*Strawberries doubled up with preserves
and topped with basil whipped cream.*

CANDY GOLD APPLE PIE

*Like a caramel apple in a crust,
only softer and sweeter.*

ALMOST MAKES YOU BELIEVE AGAIN PIE

*Poppy seeds tossed with juicy pears, tart
cranberries, and a touch of brandy.*

~

Sweet Victory Pie

MAKES ONE 9½-INCH PIE

This pie'll make people sit up straighter in their chairs—they can plainly see there's something extra-special on the plate. The lattice crust looks so beautiful and golden with all those plump red cherries peeking through. It's a pie that commands respect from the get-go.

Thing is, as stunning as it looks, this pie is dead simple. Just make sure to get good sour cherries—fresh if it's the season, or frozen if not. Jarred cherries work well, too, but be sure to drain them really well. And if you'd rather use sweet cherries like Bings and Rainiers, go right ahead; just make sure you cut back a touch on the sugar.

And don't let the lattice weave on top scare you. It may look tricky, but it's easy once you get the hang of it. Underneath it, the cherries are bursting with flavor in a syrup infused with their rich juices. Serve this up and there's nobody you can't win over. Sweet victory is as easy as pie.

Dough for a classic double-crust pie shell (page 17)

filling

5 cups pitted fresh cherries

1 cup granulated sugar

⅓ cup arrowroot starch (see page 40)

¼ teaspoon kosher salt

egg wash

1 large egg

2 tablespoons water

2 tablespoons coarse sugar, such as Demerara

---

1. **For the pie shell:** Roll out one disk of dough to a 12-inch round and fit it into a 9½-inch pie pan. There should be about ½ inch of overhang. Cover with plastic wrap and refrigerate for at least 1 hour, or until firm.

2. **For the lattice top:** Roll out the second disk of dough into a 10-inch square. Place on a sheet of parchment paper and, using a pizza cutter or a sharp knife, cut the dough into a total of eight strips that are

recipe continues

about 1½ inches wide. Cover with plastic wrap and refrigerate for at least 1 hour, or until firm.

3. Place a rimmed baking sheet in the center of the oven and preheat the oven to 350°F.

4. **For the filling:** Toss together the cherries, sugar, arrowroot, and salt in a large bowl. Pour into the pie shell.

5. Weave the chilled pastry strips into a lattice top (see "The Over and Under on Lattice Crusts," below), turn under the pastry edges, and crimp tightly. Return to the refrigerator for 15 minutes.

6. Make an egg wash by whisking together the egg and water in a small bowl. Gently brush the lattice and the crimped edge of the pie shell with the egg wash. Sprinkle the pastry with the coarse sugar.

7. Bake on the hot baking sheet for 60 to 70 minutes, or until the pastry is deep golden brown and the filling is bubbling. Place the baking sheet and pie on a wire rack to cool to room temperature.

THE OVER AND UNDER ON LATTICE CRUSTS

Making a beautiful lattice crust is a matter of folding and layering strips of dough so they appear woven, and it's not hard to do.

Roll out the dough into a 10-inch square. Use a knife, pizza cutter, or pastry wheel to cut the dough into even strips and arrange on a baking sheet; they can be narrow or wide, depending on how much filling you want to peek through. You can eyeball the strips or use a ruler to make them even (depending on your personality and patience). Chill for 10 minutes or until firm.

Arrange half the strips horizontally over the filling, spacing them evenly. Fold half of them back on themselves to expose some of the filling. Working from the center of the pie out to the edges, lay a strip of dough over the horizontal strips. Replace the folded strips over the vertical strip and fold back the alternating horizontal strips. Continue laying vertical strips over the pie and alternating which horizontal strips are flat and folded.

When all the strips are in place, trim the ends flush with the bottom crust. Fold under and crimp the edges to secure them in place. Chill the finished pie for 15 minutes before baking.

The Apple of My Eye Rum Raisin Hand Pies

I don't think you can ever have too many apple pie recipes in your file box, and these portable numbers are a rich variation on the classic. They are creamy inside, with sharp bursts of sweetness from the raisins nestled between soft, slippery slices of apple. Bake them up, and the aroma of apples, butter, and cinnamon will fill the house. They're perfect for sharing, and they keep nicely if you want to save a few for yourself. Because enjoying a pie at home makes it just about as cozy as baking one does.

filling

1/3 cup golden raisins

3 tablespoons dark rum

1 cup granulated sugar

2 tablespoons unbleached all-purpose flour

1/4 teaspoon kosher salt

1/4 teaspoon ground cinnamon

1/4 teaspoon ground mace or freshly grated nutmeg

1 cup sour cream

1 teaspoon pure vanilla extract

5 apples, peeled, cored, and cut into 1/2-inch cubes (4 cups)

Dough for a classic double-crust pie shell (page 17)

egg wash

1 large egg

2 tablespoons water

1 tablespoon coarse sugar, such as Demerara

1. Preheat the oven to 400°F. Line a rimmed baking sheet with parchment paper. ·

2. **For the filling:** Stir together the raisins and rum in a small bowl. Microwave on high for 20 seconds, then let stand until the raisins plump and absorb the rum.

3. Stir together the granulated sugar, flour, salt, cinnamon, and mace in a large bowl. Stir in the sour cream and vanilla. Fold in the apples and raisins.

4. Working with half the dough at a time, divide each dough ball into thirds. Roll each portion into a 1/8-inch-thick round

recipe continues

on a lightly floured surface. Repeat with the rest of the dough to make a total of six rounds. Divide the filling among the rounds, then fold the pastry over the filling to make half-moons. Crimp the edges tightly.

5. Make an egg wash by whisking together the egg and water in a small bowl. Gently brush the hand pies with the egg wash and sprinkle with the coarse sugar. Place the filled hand pies on the prepared baking sheet and bake in the center of the oven for 25 to 30 minutes, until deep golden brown. Place the pies, still on the baking sheet, on a wire rack to cool for 20 minutes before serving.

WASHING UP

Egg wash promotes browning and creates a bit of shine on the pastry. Be sure to beat the egg well to make the wash as thin and well mixed as possible. Adding cream gives your crust a glossier, richer sheen, while an egg-and-water wash adds a paler color; it's really a matter of preference or what you have on hand. A natural-bristle pastry brush is the best tool for brushing. Rinse the wash out of the brush immediately after use and let it dry naturally. Do not wash pastry brushes in the dishwasher, because it makes the bristles loose and misshapen.

Life's Just Peachy-Keen Polka-Dot Peach Pie

~

MAKES ONE 9½-INCH PIE

This pie is that polka-dot summer dress you only wear on the days you feel like showing off. Bursting with sugar and sunshine, this peach pie is that kind of showstopper; anyone whose head isn't turned probably wasn't your type to start with. You can't go wrong if you get fresh peaches that give you that tingle down your spine when you bite into them. Use a few for a pie now and slice up the rest to freeze for later, and the pie lovers in your life will thank you all year long for thinking ahead. And anybody else—well, who cares what they think?

Dough for a classic double-crust pie shell (page 17)

filling

6 ripe peaches, peeled, pitted, and thinly sliced (4 cups)

¼ teaspoon pure vanilla extract

¾ cup granulated sugar

¼ cup packed light brown sugar

⅓ cup arrowroot starch (see page 40)

¼ teaspoon ground cinnamon

⅛ teaspoon ground allspice

⅛ teaspoon kosher salt

egg wash

1 large egg

2 tablespoons heavy cream

2 tablespoons coarse sugar, such as Demerara

1. **For the pie shell:** Roll out one disk of dough on a lightly floured surface and fit into a 9½-inch deep-dish pie plate. Chill for at least 30 minutes, or until firm.

2. **For the top:** Roll out the second disk of dough into a 12-inch round and use a small round cutter to stamp out rounds. Cover the perforated dough and polka-dot cutouts with plastic wrap and refrigerate for at least 30 minutes, or until firm.

3. Preheat the oven to 350°F.

4. **For the filling:** Stir together the peaches and vanilla in a large bowl. Whisk together the granulated sugar, brown sugar, arrowroot, cinnamon, allspice, and salt in a small bowl, sprinkle over the peaches, and toss to coat. Pour the filling into the pie shell.

recipe continues

5. Make an egg wash by whisking together the egg and cream in a small bowl. Arrange the top crust over the filling and use the cut-out circles to decorate the edges, attaching them with a dab of egg wash. Return to the refrigerator for 15 minutes.

6. Place the pie on a rimmed baking sheet. Gently brush the pastry with the egg wash and sprinkle with the coarse sugar.

7. Bake in the center of the oven for 70 minutes, or until the crust is deep golden brown and the filling is bubbling. Place the baking sheet and pie on a wire rack to cool to room temperature.

Banish the Plum Plum Galettes

~

MAKES 6 GALETTES

My mama made hundreds of different kinds of pies, and they all had real strange names, like these little plum tarts. I know there's a story there—or maybe she just thinks personal pies are lonely. Thing about plums is, all their tartness and taste is on the skin, and they gentle into the fruit flesh as it bakes. Instead of cinnamon to spice it up, the cardamom adds a daydream of big-city sophistication. All I know is, if you make up a batch of these little beauties, people will come running to share them. Nothing lonely about that.

Dough for a classic double-crust pie shell (page 17)

filling

½ cup granulated sugar

2 tablespoons arrowroot starch (see page 40)

½ teaspoon ground cardamom

Pinch of kosher salt

1½ pounds plums, pitted and quartered (about 4 cups)

egg wash

1 large egg yolk

1 teaspoon water

1 tablespoon coarse sugar, such as Demerara

Ice cream, for serving (optional)

---

1. **For the crusts:** Line a rimmed baking sheet with parchment paper or a silicone baking mat.

2. Working with half the dough at a time, divide each dough ball into thirds. Roll each portion into a ⅛-inch-thick round on a lightly floured surface. Repeat with the rest of the dough to make a total of six rounds.

3. **For the filling:** Whisk together the granulated sugar, arrowroot, cardamom, and salt in a medium bowl. Add the plums and stir to coat.

4. Divide the plum mixture among the pastry rounds, piling it in the center of each and leaving a 1½-inch perimeter around the filling. Gather the dough up and over the edge of the fruit, pleating and pressing gently to hold it in place. Leave the galettes open in the center.

5. Make an egg wash by whisking together the egg and water in a small bowl.

recipe continues

Gently brush the pastry with the egg wash and sprinkle with the coarse sugar. Refrigerate for 15 minutes.

6. Preheat the oven to 375°F.

7. Bake the galettes in the lower third of the oven for 30 minutes, or until the pastry is golden brown and the filling bubbles. Place the baking sheet and galettes on a wire rack to cool for 15 minutes, or until the juices thicken, before serving warm, topped with ice cream, if desired.

THE THICK OF IT

Arrowroot starch (sometimes called arrowroot flour or arrowroot powder) is an effective thickener for acidic fruit pies and fillings cooked at high temperatures, although an equal amount of cornstarch will do in a pinch.

Big Guy Strawberry Pie

MAKES ONE 9½-INCH PIE

Strawberries already have a pretty big personality when you bake them into a pie, but they get a whole lot more assertive when you double them up with strawberry preserves. What you get is a pie that's extra sweet and strong enough to stand up to other flavors—like the snap of basil I snuck into the whipped cream on top. Put them all together, and these flavors make for a big taste for any big guy or gal in your life—and the smaller ones, too.

This pie is best when made with ripe strawberries, which perfume the kitchen. But if your berries are less than perfect or if you're using frozen berries, don't fret. The strawberry jam will more than make up for it.

filling

1 cup granulated sugar

½ cup arrowroot starch (see page 40)

½ teaspoon ground cinnamon

Pinch of kosher salt

1½ quarts fresh strawberries, hulled and sliced (about 5 cups)

¼ cup strawberry jam

2 tablespoons unsalted butter, cut into small cubes and chilled

Dough for a classic double-crust pie shell (page 17)

egg wash

1 large egg

2 tablespoons water

2 tablespoons coarse sugar, such as Demerara

sweet basil whipped cream

1 cup heavy cream

½ cup lightly packed fresh basil leaves and stems

2 tablespoons confectioners' sugar

Small fresh basil sprigs, for garnish

1. **For the filling:** Place a rimmed baking sheet in the oven and preheat the oven to 425°F.

2. Whisk together the granulated sugar, arrowroot, cinnamon, and salt in a large bowl. Stir in the strawberries and jam.

recipe continues

3. Roll out one disk of dough and fit it into a 9½-inch pie pan. Add the strawberry mixture and dot with butter. Roll out the other disk of dough into a 10-inch round, place over the filling, turn under the edges of the dough, and crimp the edges well.

4. Make an egg wash by whisking together the egg and water in a small bowl. Reroll any pastry scraps and cut out shapes to decorate the top crust, if desired, using a bit of the egg wash to adhere them. Gently brush the pastry with egg wash and sprinkle with the coarse sugar.

5. Bake on the baking sheet in the center of the oven for 15 minutes. Reduce the oven temperature to 350°F and bake for 30 minutes more, or until the pastry is deep golden brown and the filling is bubbling. Place the baking sheet and pie on a wire rack to cool to room temperature.

6. **For the whipped cream:** Heat the cream in a small saucepan over medium-high heat until small bubbles form around the edge. Remove the pan from the heat, rub the basil between your fingertips to bruise the leaves, and stir into the warm cream, making sure the basil is submerged. Cover and let stand at room temperature for 30 minutes. Strain into a medium bowl, pressing on the basil to extract all the cream.

7. Make an ice bath by filling a large bowl half full of ice and water. Nestle the bowl of strained cream in the ice bath and refrigerate for about 1 hour, or until chilled. Add the confectioners' sugar and use a mixer on high speed to beat the cream until it holds firm peaks.

8. Garnish each slice of pie with a dollop of the whipped cream and a small sprig of fresh basil.

Candy Gold Apple Pie

~

MAKES ONE 9½-INCH PIE

A slice of this gorgeous pie is like a caramel apple in a crust, except it's softer and even sweeter. You cook the filling on the stovetop until the apples get juicy and tender and coated in a brown sugar caramel, then add some nuts for crunch. And if that's not special enough, instead of a top crust, I bake a giant oatmeal cookie, crumble it up, and sprinkle it on top before drizzling the whole darn thing with lemony frosting. The result? Pure candy-apple joy that just about melts in your mouth.

filling

2 tablespoons unsalted butter

5 medium-size Golden Delicious apples, peeled, cored, and cut into ⅛-inch-thick slices (6 cups)

1 cup packed light brown sugar

½ cup granulated sugar

1 teaspoon ground cinnamon

½ cup hazelnuts, chopped

topping

1 cup old-fashioned rolled oats

½ teaspoon ground cinnamon

8 tablespoons (1 stick) unsalted butter, melted

½ cup sweetened condensed milk

1 cup hazelnuts, chopped

Blind-baked 9-inch pie shell (page 20), cooled to room temperature

glaze

1¼ cups confectioners' sugar

2 to 5 teaspoons fresh lemon juice

1. **For the filling:** Melt the butter in a large skillet over medium heat. Add the apples and cook for 5 minutes, or until the apples begin to soften and release their juices.

2. Stir together the brown sugar, granulated sugar, and cinnamon in a small bowl. Sprinkle over the apples and stir to coat. Cook for 10 minutes. Stir in the hazelnuts. Cook for 15 minutes more, or until the apples are tender but not falling apart. Remove from the heat and set aside.

3. Preheat the oven to 325°F. Line a rimmed baking sheet with parchment paper.

4. **For the topping:** Stir together the oats and cinnamon in a large bowl. Pour the

recipe continues

melted butter over the top and toss to coat. Stir in the sweetened condensed milk and the hazelnuts. Spread the mixture on the prepared baking sheet, as though making a big cookie. Bake for 10 minutes, or until golden. Place the baking sheet and cookie on a wire rack to cool to room temperature. Crumble the cookie into 1-inch pieces.

5. Use a slotted spoon to transfer the apples into the cooled pie shell, leaving the liquid in the skillet. Pile the crumbled cookie topping on top of the filling.

6. **For the glaze:** Whisk together the confectioners' sugar and 2 teaspoons of the lemon juice in a small bowl. The creamy glaze should be soft enough to drip off a spoon, so whisk in more lemon juice, 1 teaspoon at a time, as needed. Drizzle the glaze over the pie.

PICK A PECK OF PIE APPLES

Baking apples that hold their shape when cooked work best in pies. Those meant for eating out of hand release too much liquid and can make your pie soggy on the bottom with a runny filling. When choices are limited or if you aren't sure what type will work best, use a combination of apples; the blend of characteristics can usually compensate for any shortcomings of a variety that might not work well solo.

Almost Makes You Believe Again Pie

MAKES ONE 9½- OR 10½-INCH DEEP-DISH PIE

Reach for an ingredient long forgotten in the back of your cupboard—like poppy seeds. Something you bought but forgot you had. Toss them with juicy pears and tart cranberries, then add a touch of brandy to spice things up and some ginger so they harmonize unexpectedly.

This pie's an unlikely blind date that turns into a perfect marriage. The ingredients seem like they come from different worlds when they first meet. Then they get to know one another during the baking, and it's as if they were born to be together. If you had any doubts about what baking can do, get ready to believe.

Dough for a classic single-crust pie (page 17)

streusel

1 cup unbleached all-purpose flour

2/3 cup packed dark brown sugar

1 tablespoon poppy seeds

1 teaspoon ground ginger

1/2 teaspoon ground cinnamon

1/4 teaspoon ground cloves

1/4 teaspoon kosher salt

5 tablespoons unsalted butter, melted

1 tablespoon molasses

filling

6 pears (3 pounds), unpeeled, quartered, cored, and cut into bite-size chunks

2 cups fresh or frozen cranberries (do not thaw if frozen)

1/2 cup granulated sugar

1/4 cup minute tapioca

1 tablespoon apple cider vinegar

1 tablespoon brandy

1 tablespoon finely grated lemon zest

1 teaspoon ground cinnamon

1/2 teaspoon kosher salt

1/2 teaspoon ground ginger

1 tablespoon cold unsalted butter, cut into very small cubes

1. **For the crust:** On a lightly floured surface, roll out the dough until it is several inches larger than your pie pan, sprinkling lightly with a little more flour as needed. Transfer to a 9½- or 10½-inch deep-dish pie pan, pressing the dough into all the edges. Crimp the edges of the dough in a decorative pattern. Refrigerate until ready to fill.

2. Position a rack in the center of the oven and preheat the oven to 400°F. Place a rimmed baking sheet on the rack as it preheats.

recipe continues

3. **For the streusel:** Whisk together the flour, brown sugar, poppy seeds, ginger, cinnamon, cloves, and salt in a medium bowl. In a small bowl, whisk the melted butter and molasses to combine. Drizzle the butter mixture over the dry ingredients and stir together with a fork until small clumps form. Chill until needed.

4. **For the filling:** Combine the pears, cranberries, sugar, tapioca, vinegar, brandy, lemon zest, cinnamon, salt, and ginger in a large bowl and toss to mix well. Sprinkle the butter pieces over the filling and give it one or two folds with a rubber spatula. Pour the filling into the chilled pie crust and top with the streusel.

5. Place the pie on the baking sheet and bake for 20 minutes. Reduce the oven temperature to 375°F and bake until the filling is bubbling vigorously and the crust is baked through, 50 to 60 minutes more. Transfer to a wire rack to cool.

TURN THE HEAT AROUND

Pies can be picky about heat, and if you have had more than your share of baking mishaps, your oven may be at least partly to blame. First of all, check the temperature with an oven thermometer; your thermostat may be off by 25°F or more. Home ovens can also have hot spots, which will cause your pies to cook unevenly. If that's the case at your house, you might need to rotate the pies halfway through baking. Be sure to work quickly to avoid letting out too much heat, as that can affect baking time.

PART TWO

Dish It Up:
Savory Pies

NOT ALL PIES ARE SWEET, AND SOME DON'T EVEN HAVE A CRUST. It turns out savory pie is the answer to a whole lot of life's little problems. Like, How do I fit a meal into one easy dish? Or, How can I make dinner a day ahead so it actually tastes better when I serve it? A lot of mealtime quandaries can be solved with two words: *savory pie*. See, layering any good-tasting ingredients in a round plate and baking them transforms a normal dinner dish to *pie*. And nobody has ever complained about a pie.

Savory pies are easygoing. The crust, when they have one, is generally not all that fussy, and you can top them with anything comforting, like mashed potatoes or biscuits. These pies are some of the most comforting comfort food there is, compounded by the fact that they keep well and you won't have much to clean up when you serve them.

You can bake pretty much anything into a pie—chili, stew, huevos rancheros, jerk chicken. You can add eggs, leeks, or whatever inspires you. You can pour whatever you've got going on into a pastry shell, and with a little care and common sense, it'll come out nice. Baking simmers everything down and softens it right up. There's nothing and no one that won't get friendlier when you bake up a pie for supper.

Pie is a good way to try out unusual ingredients with picky eaters. Ingredients that might have seemed exotic, like jerk seasoning or venison, or unusual combinations like cocoa and black beans, all cozy up nicely in a pie. You don't have to tell folks whatever's under your topping unless you feel like it, because happy eaters never ask too many questions.

Try one of these pies for breakfast, lunch, dinner, or a snack. Bake it fresh or make it a day before. Whatever else you have going on in your world, savory pie will come to the rescue whenever and wherever you need it. Making pies can't solve all your problems, but they sure will make life, and supper, a wonderful thing.

~

A LITTLE WILD, WILD BERRY PIE

Venison stew, tangy blackberries, plenty of spices,
and covered with pumpkin drop biscuits.

BETRAYED BY MY EGGS PIE

Chorizo, eggs, and butter . . .
it's huevos rancheros in a crust.

LEEKY ROOF POTATO PIE

With all the bacon and cheese bubbling away
on the casserole's top,
no one will be able to resist.

MY HUSBAND'S A JERK CHICKEN POTPIE

Chicken baked with piquant spices,
peppers, and onions.

LOST SHEPHERD'S PIE

Lamb, mashed potatoes, and cheddar make a comforting,
succulent, and warm meal.

OLD JOE'S HORNY PAST PIE

A traditional Southern tomato pie—
Ritz crackers, mayonnaise, and all.

SIT ON YOUR ASS CHILI FRITO PIE

When chili sits on top of corn chips, it's officially a pie.

~

A Little Wild, Wild Berry Pie

MAKES 8 INDIVIDUAL PIES OR ONE 10-INCH SKILLET PIE

Whether you use venison or beef, this pie is a wild ride. It's got blackberries for their juicy tang, and plenty of spices: allspice, paprika, and cayenne for a fiery kick. The pumpkin drop biscuits on top may make it look domesticated, but this pie was born to be wild.

filling

1½ pounds venison shoulder or bottom round roast or beef chuck roast, cut into 2-inch pieces

2 teaspoons kosher salt, plus more as needed

1 teaspoon freshly ground black pepper, plus more as needed

1 tablespoon bacon fat or vegetable oil

1 large onion, chopped (about 3 cups)

2 tablespoons unbleached all-purpose flour

2 teaspoons paprika

½ teaspoon ground allspice

½ teaspoon cayenne pepper

2 cups pinot noir or other dry, fruity red wine

2 cups beef stock

3 garlic cloves, finely chopped

1 small sprig each fresh rosemary, sage, and thyme, plus extra thyme leaves for garnish

3 cups (1-inch cubes) peeled winter squash, such as pie pumpkin, butternut, red kuri, or kabocha

1 cup diced parsnip

1 cup diced carrot

1 pint fresh blackberries, crushed

2 tablespoons brown sugar

2 tablespoons whole-grain Dijon mustard

Juice of 1 lemon

pumpkin drop biscuit topping

2 cups unbleached all-purpose flour

1 tablespoon granulated sugar

2 teaspoons baking powder

½ teaspoon kosher salt

1 cup canned pure pumpkin puree

¾ cup heavy cream, plus more for brushing the biscuits

Coarse salt and freshly ground black pepper

1. **For the filling:** Blot the meat dry and season it with the salt and pepper. Heat the bacon fat in a Dutch oven over medium-high heat. Working in batches, add the meat and cook fir 2 to 3 minutes per side, or until deeply seared and browned, turning with tongs. Transfer the browned pieces to a bowl.

2. Add the onion and a big pinch of salt to the pot and stir to coat. If the brown glaze on the bottom of the pot begins to scorch, add a couple of tablespoons of water to loosen and stir into the onions. Cook, stirring occasionally, for 8 minutes, or until tender.

recipe continues

3. Whisk together the flour, paprika, allspice, and cayenne in a small bowl. Sprinkle over the onions and stir to coat. Cook, stirring continuously, for 2 minutes.

4. Add the wine and stir to loosen the glaze on the bottom of the pot. Stirring continuously, add the beef stock in a slow, steady stream. Bring to a simmer and cook, stirring all the while, for 3 minutes, or until thickened.

5. Return the meat and any accumulated juices to the pot. Stir in the garlic and herb sprigs. Partially cover and cook at a bare simmer for 2 hours. Add the squash, parsnip, and carrot and cook, stirring occasionally, for 30 minutes more, or until the meat and vegetables are very tender. Discard the herb stems.

6. Stir in the blackberries, brown sugar, mustard, and lemon juice and heat through. Season with salt and pepper. Keep warm over low heat.

7. Preheat the oven to 425°F.

8. **For the topping:** Whisk together the flour, sugar, baking powder, and salt in a large bowl. Whisk together the pumpkin and cream in a small bowl. Pour the pumpkin mixture into the flour mixture and stir to form a stiff dough.

9. Divide the warm filling among eight individual skillets or baking dishes that are about 5 inches in diameter. Drop a biscuit-size mound of dough evenly over the stew. Brush the tops with a little cream and sprinkle with coarse salt and pepper.

10. Bake in the center of the oven for 25 minutes, or until the biscuits are firm. Let stand for 10 minutes before serving, sprinkling each serving with fresh thyme leaves if you like.

Betrayed by My Eggs Pie

MAKES ONE 9½-INCH PIE

This is the pie you ought to eat the morning after the drinks you shouldn't have drunk the night before. Chorizo, eggs, butter, a little hair of the dog. It's huevos rancheros in a crust to set you back up after . . . Wait, what happened? I drank that? I put on my sparkly red dress? We did what? Oh, Lord. (Praying for a miracle.)

Well, whatever happened last night, and whatever happens next, at least you can count on *these* eggs for a delicious breakfast with no unplanned consequences.

spiced cornmeal pie shell

1 cup unbleached all-purpose flour

¼ cup cornmeal

1 teaspoon ground cumin

1 teaspoon chili powder

1 teaspoon sweet smoked paprika

½ teaspoon kosher salt

½ cup vegetable shortening, cut into bits and chilled

3 to 4 tablespoons ice-cold water

filling

1 pound fresh (Mexican) chorizo, casings removed

¼ cup beer

3 large eggs

½ cup red enchilada sauce

¼ cup unbleached all-purpose flour

1 teaspoon baking powder

1½ teaspoons kosher salt

1 (4-ounce) can chopped green chiles, drained

½ cup crumbled cotija cheese (2 ounces)

1. **For the pie shell:** Preheat the oven to 400°F.

2. Whisk together the flour, cornmeal, cumin, chili powder, paprika, and salt in a large bowl. Work in the shortening with a pastry blender (or pulse in the bowl of a food processor) until the mixture is crumbly. Sprinkle 3 tablespoons of the water over the flour mixture and toss with a fork (or pulse) until the mixture starts to form large clumps that pull in all the dry ingredients. Squeeze a small pinch of dough; if it is too dry to hold together, stir in more water, 1 teaspoon at a time. Pour onto a piece of plastic wrap. Gather and form into a ball, then flatten into a disk about ¾ inch thick. Wrap well and chill at least 30 minutes.

recipe continues

3. Press the dough over the bottom and up the sides of a 9½-inch pie pan. Cover with plastic wrap and refrigerate for at least 30 minutes, or until chilled. Line the pie shell with aluminum foil and fill with ½ inch of pie weights or dried beans. Bake in the upper third of the oven for 12 minutes. Fold up the corners of the foil and lift out the foil and weights. Bake for 8 minutes more, or until the pie shell is dry. Let cool to room temperature on a wire rack. Reduce the oven temperature to 350°F.

4. **For the filling:** Cook the chorizo in a large skillet over medium-high heat for 5 minutes, or until cooked through, crumbling the meat with a spoon as it cooks. Pour in the beer and cook until it has evaporated. Remove from the heat and let cool.

5. Whisk the eggs in a large bowl until the whites and yolks are well combined. Whisk in the enchilada sauce, flour, baking powder, and salt. Stir in the green chiles, ¼ cup of the cotija, and the chorizo. Pour into the pie shell.

6. Bake in the center of the oven for 30 to 35 minutes, or until set. Sprinkle with the remaining ¼ cup cotija cheese and let stand for 10 minutes on a wire rack. Serve warm.

Leeky Roof Potato Pie

MAKES ONE 9½-INCH PIE

This supper pie fixes a whole mess of problems. Make it when your house needs the dreamy aroma of leeks and sweet potatoes to make it smell properly like a home. With all the bacon and cheese bubbling away on the casserole's top, no one will be able to resist. The rain's going to fall when it falls, but baking this pie will keep you happy and warm.

sliced sweet potato pie shell

- 2 small, slender sweet potatoes (6 to 8 ounces each)
- 2 tablespoons unsalted butter, melted

filling

- 6 ounces thick bacon slices, cut crosswise into ½-inch strips
- 2 medium leeks, white and tender green parts only, cleaned well and thinly sliced (about 1½ cups)
- 1 teaspoon chopped fresh thyme leaves
- 1 cup freshly shredded Gruyère cheese (4 ounces)
- 1¼ cups half-and-half
- 2 large eggs
- 1 large egg yolk
- 1 teaspoon kosher salt
- ½ teaspoon freshly ground black pepper
- ½ teaspoon dry mustard
- ½ teaspoon freshly grated nutmeg

1. **For the pie shell:** Preheat the oven to 375°F.

2. Peel the potatoes and use a mandoline or vegetable slicer to cut them crosswise into very thin rounds. Place in a large glass bowl, fill with water, and cover with plastic wrap. Microwave on high for 3 to 5 minutes, or until the sweet potatoes are tender but not breaking apart. Uncover, carefully pour off any liquid, and let stand until cool enough to handle.

3. Brush a 9½-inch pie plate with the butter. Arrange the sweet potato rounds over the bottom and up the sides of the pie plate, overlapping the edges and pressing gently to help them stay in place. Gently brush with melted butter. Bake in the upper third of the oven until the potatoes begin to dry and brown a bit along the top edges, about 20 minutes. Let cool on a wire rack. If the potato rounds slip down as they cool, gently push and press them

recipe continues

back into place with the back of a spoon. Keep the oven on.

4. **For the filling:** Cook the bacon in a large skillet over medium heat, stirring occasionally, for 20 minutes, or until it is crisp and the fat has been rendered. Transfer to paper towels to drain and cool.

5. Pour off all but 1 tablespoon of the fat from the skillet. Add the leeks and stir to coat in the fat. Cook, stirring often, for 5 minutes, or until tender but not browned. Stir in the thyme. Transfer to a medium bowl and let cool. Stir in the bacon and the Gruyère. Pour into the pie shell.

6. Whisk together the half-and-half, eggs, egg yolk, salt, pepper, dry mustard, and nutmeg until well blended. Pour slowly over the leek mixture.

7. Bake in the center of the oven for 30 minutes, or until the filling is golden brown and set. Place on a wire rack to cool for at least 30 minute before serving just warm to the touch or at room temperature.

MAKE IT UP
AND SURPRISE THEM

TELL THEM ALL MY SECRETS
BUT DISGUISE THEM

SO THEY DANCE ON THE
TONGUES OF THE VERY OOH . . .

PEOPLE THAT THEY'RE
SECRETS FROM

My Husband's a Jerk Chicken Potpie

MAKES ONE 9½-INCH PIE

Baking is a perfect way to work out the stresses of the day, and this recipe works like a charm. Pound chicken till it's unrecognizable. Pack flour quickly. Use only essential ingredients. Simmer without a lid, enabling the vapor to escape swiftly from the mixture. Add piquant spices and peppers and onion and simmer it into a delicious spicy gravy. And when they ask what it's called, just smile.

top crust

- 1 cup unbleached all-purpose flour
- 1 teaspoon sugar
- ½ teaspoon baking powder
- ½ teaspoon kosher salt
- 4 tablespoons (½ stick) unsalted butter, cut into cubes and chilled
- 2 tablespoons vegetable shortening, cut into bits and chilled
- 1 large egg
- 2 teaspoons distilled white vinegar
- 1 to 1½ tablespoons ice-cold water

filling

- 1½ tablespoons vegetable oil
- 8 ounces long, slender sweet potatoes, peeled and cut into 1-inch cubes (about 2 cups)
- ½ cup chopped onion
- ¼ cup diced red bell pepper
- ½ teaspoon kosher salt, plus more as needed
- 3 teaspoons jerk seasoning paste
- 1 pound boneless, skinless chicken thighs
- 2 tablespoons unsalted butter
- 2 tablespoons unbleached all-purpose flour
- 1 cup chicken stock
- 2 tablespoons heavy cream
- ½ cup frozen baby green peas, thawed
- ¾ cup cooked and cooled long-grain white rice
- Freshly ground black pepper
- 2 tablespoons chopped fresh flat-leaf parsley

egg wash

- 1 large egg
- 2 tablespoons heavy cream
- Coarse salt and freshly cracked black pepper

1. **For the top crust:** Whisk together the flour, sugar, baking powder, and salt in a large bowl. Scatter the butter and shortening over the flour mixture and work it in with a pastry blender (or pulse

recipe continues

in the bowl of a food processor) until the mixture is crumbly with a few pieces of butter the size of small peas.

2. Whisk together the egg, vinegar, and 1 tablespoon of the water in a small bowl, whisking until there are no long strands of egg white. Pour over the flour mixture. Stir with a fork (or pulse in the bowl of a food processor) to form large clumps that pull in all the dry ingredients. Squeeze a small pinch of dough; if it's too dry to hold together, stir in more of the water, 1 teaspoon at a time. Turn out onto a piece of plastic wrap. Gather and form into a ball and then flatten into a disk about ¾ inch thick. Wrap well and refrigerate for at least 30 minutes.

3. Preheat the oven to 400°F. Lightly grease a 9½-inch deep-dish pie pan with nonstick cooking spray.

4. **For the filling:** Heat 1 tablespoon of the oil in a large pot over medium-high heat. Stir in the sweet potatoes, onion, bell pepper, and salt. Cook, stirring occasionally, for 8 minutes, or until tender. Stir in 1 teaspoon of the jerk seasoning and transfer to a large bowl; set aside.

5. Heat the remaining 1½ teaspoons oil in the same pot. Toss the chicken with 1 teaspoon of the jerk seasoning and arrange in a single layer in the pot. Cook for 3 minutes on each side, or until lightly browned, turning with tongs. Transfer to a plate; set aside.

6. Reduce the heat to medium-low and melt the butter in the pot. Sprinkle the flour over the butter and cook, whisking continuously, for 2 minutes. Whisk in the stock and cook for 4 minutes, or until slightly thickened. Whisk in the cream and the remaining 1 teaspoon jerk seasoning paste.

7. Cut the chicken into bite-size pieces and add to the pot along with any accumulated juices. Stir in the reserved vegetables, peas, and rice. Cook until gently bubbling and heated through. Season with salt and pepper. Stir in the parsley. Transfer to the prepared pie plate.

8. Roll out the dough to a 10-inch round on a lightly floured surface. Cover the filling with the dough and crimp the edge. (If you have any pastry scraps, you can cut out shapes to decorate the crust.)

9. Make an egg wash by whisking together the egg and cream in a small bowl. Gently brush the dough with egg wash and sprinkle with coarse salt and cracked pepper. Cut four 1-inch slits in the pastry to vent the steam.

10. Place the pie plate on a rimmed baking sheet. Bake for about 45 minutes, or until the crust is golden brown and the filling is bubbling. Let stand for 15 minutes before serving.

Lost Shepherd's Pie

MAKES ONE 9½-INCH PIE

Lamb, for the little child who ran into the diner one time. Mashed potatoes, to comfort the haggard mother who came trailing behind. A food mill, for what that boy put his mama through all during lunch, banging and whining and carrying on. Warm milk, for when she turned to me and said, "They never tell you how damned hard it's gonna be." Cheddar, for the meltdown we could all see coming.

That's my Lost Shepherd's Pie: a comforting, succulent, and warm meal, inspired by and meant for all the tired mamas with Silly String stuck in their hair.

mashed potato and cheddar topping

1¼ pounds russet potatoes, peeled and cut into 2-inch chunks

2 ounces cream cheese, at room temperature

2 tablespoons unsalted butter, at room temperature

1 large egg yolk, lightly beaten

¼ cup whole milk, warmed

¾ cup freshly shredded sharp cheddar cheese

Kosher salt and freshly ground black pepper

filling

1 tablespoon vegetable oil

1 pound lean ground lamb, meat loaf mix, or ground beef

1 tablespoon unsalted butter

1 small onion, chopped (about 1 cup)

Kosher salt

1 garlic clove, finely chopped

1 tablespoon tomato paste

2 tablespoons unbleached all-purpose flour

½ cup dry red wine

2 tablespoons Worcestershire sauce

¾ cup beef stock

1 cup frozen mixed baby green peas and diced carrots, thawed

1 tablespoon A.1. steak sauce

2 teaspoons fresh thyme leaves

Freshly ground black pepper

1. **For the topping:** Simmer the potatoes in a large pot of generously salted water over medium-high heat for 20 minutes, or until just tender; do not let the potatoes break apart or get waterlogged. Drain well in a colander, then return to the pot and let stand for 5 minutes, or until the potatoes steam dry and the edges look chalky. Pass the warm potatoes through a food mill or ricer into a large bowl.

recipe continues

(Alternatively, mash the potatoes as smooth as possible with a potato masher or large spoon. Do not process, blend, or beat the potatoes, as this will cause them to become gluey.)

2. Stir the cream cheese, butter, and egg yolk into the warm potatoes. Stir in the milk and cheddar. Season with salt and pepper. Cover and set aside.

3. Preheat the oven to 400°F. Spray a 9½-inch deep-dish pie pan with nonstick cooking spray.

4. **For the filling:** Heat the oil in large skillet over medium-high heat. Add the meat and cook, stirring to crumble, for about 5 minutes, or until no longer pink. Transfer the meat to a colander to drain, then set aside.

5. Melt the butter in the same skillet over medium-high heat. Stir in the onion and a big pinch of salt. Cook, stirring occasionally, for 5 minutes, or until tender. Stir in the garlic. Return the meat to the pan and raise the heat to high; when the onion mixture begins to sizzle, quickly stir in the tomato paste. Cook for 30 seconds, stirring continuously.

6. Reduce the heat to medium-high. Sprinkle the flour over the onion mixture and stir to coat. Cook, stirring continuously, for 2 minutes.

7. Add the wine and Worcestershire sauce and stir to loosen the glaze on the bottom of the pot.

8. Stirring continuously, add the beef stock in a slow, steady stream. Bring to a simmer over medium heat and cook, gently stirring continuously, for 3 minutes, or until thickened.

9. Stir in the peas and carrots. Simmer for 10 minutes. Stir in the A.1. and thyme. Season with salt and pepper. Transfer to the prepared pie plate. Spoon the mashed potato topping over the filling and rough up the top a bit with a fork. Bake in the upper third of the oven for 30 minutes, or until browned in spots on top.

NOTE: *To get a fancy, lattice-like effect on your pie, spoon the mashed potatoes into a pastry bag fitted with a ribbon or basketweave tip. (You may have some potatoes left over; cover and save for another meal or reheat and serve on the side.) Pipe three or four rows in each direction.*

Old Joe's Horny Past Pie

Joe, the owner of the diner where I work, comes in every morning and usually tells me a lot more than just his breakfast order. He'll give me an earful about his horoscope, or how the heat's too darn high, or a story about how you remind him of that girl he "made sweet love to in the summer of 1948." Yessireebub.

He's an old-fashioned fella, so I made him a traditional Southern tomato pie—Ritz crackers, mayonnaise, and all. Except instead of cheddar, I added goat cheese, because he's an old goat. Just make sure you make it the night before since, just like old Joe, you'll want it to cool down before you serve it.

cracker crumb pie shell

- 1¾ cups Ritz or saltine cracker crumbs
- 6 tablespoons (¾ stick) unsalted butter, melted

filling

- 2 pounds large, sun-ripened tomatoes, preferably a mix of red and yellow
- ½ teaspoon kosher salt, plus more as needed
- ½ cup mayonnaise
- 2 tablespoons finely chopped scallions
- Finely grated zest of 1 lemon
- 1 tablespoon fresh lemon juice
- ¼ teaspoon celery seed
- ¼ teaspoon freshly ground black pepper, or to taste
- ½ cup crumbled fresh goat cheese
- 3 tablespoons lightly packed coarsely chopped fresh basil leaves, plus a handful of small leaves for garnish
- ½ cup coarsely crushed Ritz or saltine cracker crumbs
- ⅓ cup freshly shredded Parmesan cheese
- 1 tablespoon unsalted butter, melted

1. **For the pie shell:** Preheat the oven to 350°F. Toss together the crumbs and butter in a medium bowl to moisten. Press the mixture onto the bottom and up the sides of a 9½-inch pie pan. Refrigerate for at least 15 minutes to firm up the butter. Bake in the center of the oven for about 10 minutes, or until just set and fragrant. Place on a wire rack to cool to room temperature.

recipe continues

2. **For the filling:** Preheat the oven to 350°F. Use a serrated knife to cut the tomatoes crosswise into ¼-inch-thick rounds. Cover a wire rack with a double layer of paper towels and set the rack over the sink to catch any drips. Arrange the tomato slices in a single layer on the paper towels. Sprinkle them with the salt and let drain for at least 15 minutes. Blot the tomatoes dry with more paper towels. Arrange half the sliced tomatoes in the pie shell.

3. Stir together the mayonnaise, scallions, lemon zest and juice, celery seed, pepper, and goat cheese in a medium bowl. Spread over the tomatoes. Sprinkle with the basil. Arrange the remaining tomatoes over the basil.

4. Toss together the crumbs, Parmesan, and butter in a small bowl and then sprinkle over the pie.

5. Bake in the center of the oven for 30 minutes, or until the top is browned. Let cool to room temperature on a wire rack and then cover and refrigerate until chilled. Serve garnished with fresh basil leaves.

Sit on Your Ass Chili Frito Pie

~

SERVES 8

There's a pie for every kind of day, even the kind of day when you've already been on your feet for eight hours straight.

First, do some quick chopping and set a pot of fixings for rich, spicy chili on the stove. Now you can sit for a minute. Then pour a little beer into your mixture, and go back to your chair to finish the bottle. When the chili's done, ladle it right into a bag of chips—no crust, no cleanup, no more getting out of that chair.

Yes, this is a real pie. You could have simply put chips in chili, but that's just chili. When the chili sits on top of the chips, that's officially a pie. Okay, now go take a load off.

---

chili filling

1 tablespoon vegetable oil

1½ pounds ground chuck or ground dark-meat turkey

1 large onion, chopped (about 3 cups)

1 teaspoon kosher salt, plus more as needed

½ cup tomato paste

2 garlic cloves, finely chopped

3 tablespoons premium chili powder

1½ teaspoons ground cumin

1½ teaspoons dried Mexican oregano

1½ teaspoons unsweetened cocoa powder

1 cup dark beer

1 cup beef stock

1 (14.5-ounce) can petite diced tomatoes with their juices

1 (14.5-ounce) can black or pinto beans, drained

Juice of 2 limes

8 individual packages or 1 large bag corn chips, preferably Fritos

toppings

Shredded cheese, sour cream, pickled jalapeños

---

1. **For the filling:** Heat the oil in a large saucepan over medium-high heat. Stir in the ground meat and cook for 5 minutes, or until there are no traces of pink, stirring to break it up. Use a slotted spoon to transfer to a bowl.

2. Add the onion and salt to the pan and stir to coat the onion in the drippings (or heat a little more oil if the drippings are skimpy and the pan is dry); cook, stirring occasionally, for 5 minutes, or until tender. Raise the heat to high; as

recipe continues

soon as the onion begins to sizzle, stir in the tomato paste and cook, stirring continuously, for 30 seconds. Stir in the garlic, chili powder, cumin, oregano, and cocoa powder. Cook, stirring continuously, for 1 minute. Reduce the heat if the spices start to stick or scorch.

3. Add the beer and beef stock and stir to loosen the browned bits and glaze from the bottom of the pot. Return the meat to the pot. Cover and simmer over low heat for 30 minutes.

4. Stir in the tomatoes and beans and simmer for 10 minutes. Check the seasoning. Stir in the lime juice.

5. Split open the bags of Fritos to create bowls of sorts (or divide the large bag of chips among serving bowls). Spoon the chili over the chips. Top with cheese, sour cream, and jalapeños and serve at once.

SPICE THINGS UP

Dried herbs and spices last only about a year once opened, even less if they are exposed to excessive heat and humidity. Give your spices a sniff from time to time. If their aroma has faded away, so has their flavor, and they are adding little more than dust to your recipes.

PART THREE

Feels So Good to Be Bad: Chocolate and Nut Pies

CHOCOLATE IS A TREAT ANY OLD DAY, BUT CHOCOLATE *PIE* MAKES an occasion special. Chocolate pie says "celebration," "congratulations," or "hot date" like nothing else. You can serve any other kind of pie at dinner and you won't raise an eyebrow, but chocolate pie is definitely going to raise expectations. It's sort of the "hip-hip-hooray" of pies.

Now, to my mind, the more chocolate, the better. There's no good reason to limit it to the filling. You can go wild with a chocolate crumb crust, bonus hidden filling, or chocolate curls. All these pies make for a deep flavor that supports added layers of richness, like chocolate-covered strawberries or a shot of bourbon. Once you start adding extras to a chocolate pie, it's hard to stop—and there's nothing that says you have to.

I don't think there's a person alive who's immune to the seductions of an intense chocolate pie. Don't be afraid to use dark chocolate. The sugar will balance its bitter qualities, and the intensity adds depth and makes it kind of sultry. I always keep a bag of dark chocolate chips on hand for emergency chocolate-pie baking but when I have a little more time I go for a chunk of the good stuff and chop it into bits with a big, sharp kitchen knife. Chocolate with 70% or more cacao is best for delivering a full-blown blast of chocolate flavor, and when it comes to chocolate, why be timid?

Don't expect to cut yourself a tiny sliver of chocolate pie and leave it at that, because these pies are going to taste like more. It only takes one bite and you'll want the whole thing. Not that I'd ever try to seduce anyone with a chocolate pie! But you know, a person could.

~

I WANNA PLAY DOCTOR WITH MY GYNECOLOGIST CHOCOLATE MOUSSE PIE

It's got the charms of chocolate, a touch of liqueur, and soft, sweet cherries bursting all over.

JENNA'S DEVIL'S FOOD CHOCOLATE OASIS PIE

Flooded with chocolate and strawberry and topped with a dreamy sweet cloud of whipped cream.

IN THE DARK DARK TRIPLE CHOCOLATE TRUFFLE PIE

A warm embrace of chocolate and a bed of creamy soft filling.

TWISTED KENTUCKY BOURBON PECAN PIE

Like a stiff cocktail, with a zing of bourbon, bitters, and orange, all in a solid cornmeal shell.

SLOW AS MOLASSES SHOOFLY PIE

A rich, gooey delight, sort of a pecan pie without the nuts.

I CAN'T HAVE AN AFFAIR BECAUSE IT'S WRONG (AND I DON'T WANT EARL TO KILL ME) MARBLED CHOCOLATE CHEESECAKE PIE

Velvety white chocolate cheesecake with ripples of devilishly dark chocolate swirled right in.

~

I Wanna Play Doctor with My Gynecologist Chocolate Mousse Pie

MAKES ONE 9½-INCH PIE

This pie knows right where your sweet spot is. I came up with the recipe in a moment of, let's just say, great temptation in my personal life. It's got all the charms of chocolate to pull you in, a touch of liquor to break down your resistance, and before you can stop yourself, you've got soft, sweet cherries busting out all over. Sometimes you gotta let yourself go, I guess. Watch out, is all I'm saying.

shortbread cookie pie shell

1¾ cups shortbread cookie crumbs (about 8 cookies)

6 tablespoons (¾ stick) unsalted butter, melted

cherry filling

1 pound pitted fresh or frozen sweet cherries, thawed and drained

Juice of 1 lemon (about 2 tablespoons)

2 tablespoons cornstarch

¼ cup granulated sugar

1 teaspoon almond extract

chocolate mousse filling

5 ounces semisweet chocolate, chopped

¾ cup heavy cream

3 large egg whites, at room temperature

chocolate-covered cherries

8 ounces semisweet chocolate chips

1 heaping tablespoon vegetable shortening

20 maraschino cherries with stems

whipped cream topping

1 cup heavy cream, chilled

¼ cup confectioners' sugar

1 tablespoon bourbon

1 teaspoon vanilla extract

1. **For the pie shell:** Preheat the oven to 350°F. Toss together the crumbs and butter in a medium bowl to moisten. Press the mixture onto the bottom and up the sides of a 9½-inch deep-dish pie pan. Refrigerate for at least 15 minutes to firm up the butter. Bake in the center of the oven for about 10 minutes, or until just set and fragrant. Let cool to room temperature on a wire rack.

2. **For the cherry filling:** Stir together the cherries and lemon juice in a medium

recipe continues

saucepan. Sprinkle with the cornstarch and sugar and stir to coat. Bring to a boil over medium-high heat while stirring continuously. Cook for 1 minute, or until thickened. Remove from the heat and stir in the almond extract. Pour into the pie shell and refrigerate for 30 minutes, or until set.

3. **For the chocolate mousse filling:** Set up a double boiler or place a metal bowl over a saucepan and bring the water in the bottom pan to a simmer (do not let the water touch the bottom of the bowl). Place the chocolate and ¼ cup of the cream in the bowl and stir occasionally until smooth. Set aside to cool to room temperature.

4. In a large bowling using a mixer, beat the egg whites on high speed until they hold stiff peaks. Fold one-third of the whites into the chocolate to lighten, and then fold in the rest of the whites.

5. Beat the remaining ½ cup cream to stiff peaks in a medium bowl with a mixer set to high speed. Fold into the egg white

mixture. Pour over the cherry filling and smooth the top. Refrigerate for at least 4 hours, or until set.

6. **For the cherries:** Place the chocolate chips and shortening in a medium glass bowl. Microwave on 50 percent power in 30-second intervals until the chips begin to lose their shape. Stir until melted and smooth.

7. Drain the cherries and blot dry. Holding the cherries by the stem end, dip one at a time into the chocolate, letting any excess drip back into the bowl. Place the coated cherries on a plate lined with parchment or waxed paper. Refrigerate for about 30 minutes, or until the chocolate hardens.

8. **For the topping:** Combine the cream, confectioners' sugar, bourbon, and vanilla in a chilled medium bowl. With a mixer, beat on high speed until it holds firm peaks. Spoon the whipped cream around the edge of the chilled pie. Garnish the whipped cream with the chocolate-covered cherries.

DOUBLE, DOUBLE, BOIL AND BUBBLE

If you don't own a double boiler, it's easy to improvise one by setting a metal bowl over a saucepan. Fill the saucepan about one-third full of water and bring to a simmer, not a full boil. Set a metal bowl on top; the bottom of the bowl should not touch the hot water. The warm air between the simmering water and the bowl insulates your mixture from excess heat and prevents eggs from scrambling, custards from scorching, and chocolate from burning or seizing.

Jenna's Devil's Food Chocolate Oasis Pie

～

MAKES ONE 9½-INCH PIE

This one is a thing of beauty. The flavors open themselves one by one, like chapters in a book. First you get flooded with chocolate, dark and bittersweet like an old flame with a hint of balsamic. And then strawberry, its sweetness hidden under a cloak of semisweet chocolate and nestled in a dreamy sweet cloud of whipped cream.

A customer once called this is a perfect pie. I don't know about that, but it's certainly a pie you won't mind getting a little lost in.

chocolate cookie crumb pie shell

1¾ cups chocolate wafer cookie crumbs (about 36 cookies)

6 tablespoons (¾ stick) unsalted butter, melted

chocolate cream filling

½ cup strawberry preserves

2 tablespoons aged balsamic vinegar

⅔ cup granulated sugar

¼ cup cornstarch

½ teaspoon kosher salt

4 large egg yolks

3 cups whole milk

7 ounces bittersweet chocolate, chopped

2 tablespoons unsalted butter, at room temperature

1 teaspoon pure vanilla extract

chocolate-covered strawberries

8 ounces semisweet chocolate chips

1 heaping tablespoon vegetable shortening

16 large fresh strawberries, hulled

strawberry whipped cream topping

1 cup heavy cream, chilled

2 tablespoons confectioners' sugar

⅓ cup crushed fresh strawberries

1. **For the pie shell:** Preheat the oven to 350°F. Toss together the crumbs and butter in a medium bowl to moisten. Press the mixture onto the bottom and up the sides of a 9½-inch deep-dish pie pan. Refrigerate for at least 15 minutes to firm up the butter. Bake in the center of the oven for about 10 minutes, or until just set and fragrant. Place on a wire rack to cool to room temperature.

recipe continues

2. **For the filling:** Stir together the preserves and vinegar in a small bowl. Spread over the bottom of the chilled crust and return to the refrigerator.

3. Whisk together the granulated sugar, cornstarch, salt, and egg yolks in a large, heavy saucepan. While whisking continuously, add the milk in a slow, steady stream. Bring to a boil over medium heat, whisking, then reduce the heat and simmer, whisking, for 1 minute, or until the filling is very thick. Remove from the heat, add the chocolate, butter, and vanilla, and stir until smooth.

4. Pass the pastry cream through a fine-mesh sieve into a glass or metal bowl, using a rubber spatula to press it through the mesh. Press a piece of buttered parchment paper directly onto the surface to prevent a skin from forming. Let cool to room temperature and then pour the filling into the crust. Refrigerate at least 6 hours, or until fully set.

5. **For the berries:** Place the chocolate chips and shortening in a medium glass bowl. Microwave on 50 percent power in 30-second intervals until the chips begin to lose their shape. Stir until melted and smooth.

6. Rinse the berries and blot dry. Holding the berries by the stem end, dip them one at a time into the chocolate, letting any excess drip back into the bowl. Place the coated berries on a plate lined with parchment or waxed paper. Refrigerate for about 30 minutes, or until the chocolate hardens.

7. **For the topping:** In a medium bowl using a mixer, beat the cream and confectioners' sugar on high speed until it holds firm peaks. Fold in the crushed strawberries. Spread over the chilled pie. Arrange the chocolate-covered strawberries on top.

BETTER BUTTER

To achieve that just-right stage for room temperature or softened butter, leave it in a cool, shaded spot on the kitchen counter for 2 hours. Test the softness by pressing the butter with your finger; if the indention shows but the butter holds its shape, it's perfect. If you forget to set out the butter and need to resort to the microwave, use the lowest power level and heat the butter in 10-second intervals. Overly soft or melted butter will not work properly in recipes that call for room-temperature butter, even if you let it solidify again.

In the Dark Dark Triple Chocolate Truffle Pie

~

MAKES ONE 9½-INCH PIE

This is the best bad idea I've had in so long.

A little taste becomes too much of a good thing awful quick. But here, I'm inventing a recipe: a deep, warm embrace of chocolate; a teasing, gentle bite of cocoa; a bed of creamy soft filling. Floating happily in darkness you can't see through, can't see the bottom, can't see anything farther than the next stolen mouthful. Careful, it'll leave a trace on your cheek. Wipe it away and take one more bite.

---

chocolate cookie pie shell

1¾ cups chocolate wafer cookie crumbs (about 36 cookies)

6 tablespoons (¾ stick) unsalted butter, melted

filling

8 ounces bittersweet chocolate, chopped

2 cups half-and-half

2 large eggs

chocolate whipped cream topping

1 cup heavy cream, chilled

1 teaspoon pure vanilla extract

¼ cup confectioners' sugar

3 tablespoons unsweetened cocoa powder

chocolate curls

1 (2-ounce) block dark chocolate

1 (2-ounce) block white chocolate

---

1. **For the pie shell:** Preheat the oven to 350°F. Toss together the crumbs and butter in a medium bowl to moisten. Press the mixture onto the bottom and up the sides of a 9½-inch deep-dish pie pan. Refrigerate for at least 15 minutes to firm up the butter. Bake in the center of the oven for about 10 minutes, or until just set and fragrant. Place on a wire rack to cool to room temperature.

2. **For the filling:** Place the chopped chocolate in a medium heatproof bowl. Warm the half-and-half in a small

recipe continues

saucepan over medium heat until small bubbles form around the edge. Pour over the chocolate and let stand for 1 minute to soften, then whisk until smooth.

3. Whisk the eggs in a medium bowl until the whites and yolks are well combined. Whisking continuously, add the warm chocolate mixture to the eggs in ¼-cup increments. Pour into the pie shell.

4. Bake in the center of the oven for 45 minutes, or until the filling is nearly set in the center and puffs slightly. When gently shaken, the center should jiggle slightly, but no longer slosh or ripple, and a toothpick inserted 3 inches from the center should come out clean. The center of the pie will firm up as it cools. Place the baking sheet and pie on a wire rack to cool to room temperature.

5. **For the topping:** Whisk together the cream, vanilla, confectioners' sugar, and cocoa powder in a large chilled bowl until the dry ingredients mix into the cream. Beat to firm peaks with a mixer on high speed. Spread over the filling, or pipe onto the pie in a decorative fashion using a large star tip.

6. **For the chocolate curls:** Soften the dark chocolate in the microwave on 50 percent power in 10-second intervals until it is slightly warmer than room temperature but not melting or soft enough to show fingerprints. For wide curls, slowly draw the blade of a vegetable peeler along the broad side of the softened chocolate to create curls. For narrow curls, use the side of the block. Repeat with the white chocolate.

7. Use the curls immediately or arrange them in a single layer on a sheet of parchment paper in an airtight storage container. Refrigerate the curls until ready to use. Chilled curls shatter easily, so handle them gently.

Twisted Kentucky Bourbon Pecan Pie

MAKES ONE 9½-INCH PIE

This pie is not your standard pecan pie, the kind that's like a pleasant cousin you're on friendly terms with. No, this pie is your loud, loyal best friend. She's a little bit nuts, on account of the pecans. She's also sweet as hell. But what makes her special is how she kicks like a stiff cocktail, with a zing of bourbon, bitters, and orange. All that in a solid cornmeal shell. This is the pie to set you straight no matter what may befall you.

This crust is a bit crumbly and needs to be handled with special care. If you have any extra after lining the pan, twist two strips into a rope to decorate the edge of the pie. But, like your friend, you don't want to give it *too* much rope.

cornmeal pie shell

- ¾ cup unbleached all-purpose flour
- ½ cup plain white cornmeal
- ¼ cup confectioners' sugar
- 1 teaspoon finely grated orange zest
- ¼ teaspoon kosher salt
- 6 tablespoons (¾ stick) unsalted butter, cut into cubes and chilled
- 2 tablespoons vegetable shortening, cut into bits and chilled
- 3 to 4 tablespoons ice-cold water

filling

- 6 tablespoons (¾ stick) unsalted butter
- 1¼ cups packed light brown sugar
- ½ cup light corn syrup
- ¼ cup honey
- 3 tablespoons bourbon
- 2 teaspoons pure vanilla extract
- 1 teaspoon Angostura bitters
- ½ teaspoon finely grated orange zest
- ¼ teaspoon kosher salt
- 3 large eggs, lightly beaten
- 1 tablespoon unbleached all-purpose flour
- 2 cups pecan pieces

bourbon whipped cream topping

- 1 cup heavy cream, chilled
- ¼ cup confectioners' sugar
- 1 tablespoon bourbon
- 1 teaspoon pure vanilla extract

recipe continues

1. **For the pie shell:** Whisk together the flour, cornmeal, confectioners' sugar, orange zest, and salt in a large bowl. Sprinkle the butter and shortening over the flour mixture and work it in with a pastry blender (or pulse in the bowl of a food processor) until the mixture is crumbly with a few pieces of butter the size of small peas. Sprinkle 3 tablespoons of the water over the flour mixture and stir with a fork (or pulse in the bowl of a food processor) until the mixture forms large clumps that pull in all the dry ingredients. Squeeze a small pinch of dough; if it is too dry to hold together, stir in more water, 1 teaspoon at a time. Pour onto a piece of plastic wrap. Gather and form into a ball, then flatten into a disk about ¾ inch thick. Wrap well and chill for 30 minutes.

2. Roll the dough on a lightly floured surface with a lightly floured pin to a 12-inch round. Fit into a 9½-inch deep-dish pie plate, leaving a ½-inch overhang. Fold the edges under and crimp as desired. Chill for at least 30 minutes, or until firm.

3. **For the filling:** Place a rimmed baking sheet in the center of the oven and preheat the oven to 350°F.

4. Melt the butter in a large saucepan over medium heat. Add the brown sugar and whisk until smooth. Remove the pan from the heat and whisk in the corn syrup, honey, bourbon, vanilla, bitters, orange zest, and salt. Whisk in the eggs and then the flour. Stir in the pecans. Pour into the pie shell.

5. Place the pie on the hot baking sheet and bake for 50 to 60 minutes, or until the filling is nearly set in the center and slightly puffed. When gently shaken, the center should jiggle slightly but no longer slosh or ripple, and a toothpick inserted 3 inches from the center should come out clean. The center of the pie will firm up as it cools. Place the baking sheet and pie on a wire rack to cool to room temperature.

6. **For the topping:** Combine the cream, confectioners' sugar, bourbon, and vanilla in a chilled medium bowl. Beat to firm peaks with a mixer on high speed. Spoon the whipped cream around the edge of the chilled pie.

TAKE A SHEET

It's hard to get a crisp, brown bottom crust on a pie with a very juicy filling; too often they come out underbaked, with a flabby, soggy bottom. And no one wants that in a pie. To give the bottom crust a bit of a head start, place a baking sheet in the oven as it preheats. When the filled pie is ready to bake, place it directly on the hot baking sheet. This will help the bottom crust firm up and brown.

Slow as Molasses Shoofly Pie

MAKES ONE 9½-INCH PIE

Sometimes only an old standby will do, a humble dessert you can rely on even when there's not much in the cupboard. Shoofly pie is a rich, gooey delight, sort of like a pecan pie without the nuts. Some like a crumb topping but go for a dreamy caramel sauce instead. I make this pie when I want to slow the world down. It's best accompanied by some coffee and a long conversation. This pie doesn't actually take long to make; it's just worth savoring real, real slow.

caramel

1 cup granulated sugar

¼ cup packed brown sugar

2 tablespoons water

8 tablespoons (1 stick) unsalted butter

½ cup heavy cream, at room temperature

1 teaspoon kosher salt

filling

1 cup unbleached all-purpose flour

1 cup packed dark brown sugar

1 teaspoon ground ginger

½ teaspoon ground allspice

¼ teaspoon kosher salt

3 tablespoons unsalted butter, cut into small cubes and chilled

¾ cup blackstrap molasses

¼ cup dark corn syrup

1 tablespoon apple cider vinegar

1 large egg

1 cup boiling water

1 teaspoon baking soda

9½-inch partially blind-baked pie shell, (page 20), cooled to room temperature

1. **For the caramel:** Whisk together the granulated sugar, brown sugar, and water in a small saucepan. Add the butter and cook over medium-low heat until the butter melts and then whisk until smooth. Raise the heat to medium and bring to a boil. Let boil for 8 minutes, or until the caramel darkens a few shades and thickens slightly.

2. Remove the pan from the heat and slowly pour in the cream. The mixture will bubble vigorously and might harden in spots. Return to the heat and stir until smooth. Stir in the salt. Set aside to cool slightly and then pour into a glass jar or bowl and set aside to cool to room temperature. (The caramel will keep,

recipe continues

covered and refrigerated, for up to 3 days. Return to room temperature for serving.)

3. Preheat the oven to 325°F.

4. **For the filling:** Make a crumble by whisking together the flour, brown sugar, ginger, allspice, and salt in a medium bowl. Work in the butter with your fingertips or a pastry blender until the mixture resembles coarse sand and a small bit pinched together holds its shape. Set aside.

5. Whisk together the molasses, corn syrup, vinegar, and egg in a large bowl.

6. Stir together the boiling water and baking soda in a heatproof liquid measuring cup with a pouring spout, stirring until the baking soda dissolves, and then pour it into the molasses mixture and whisk until smooth. Pour into the pie shell. Sprinkle the crumble mixture over the filling; it will sink into the filling (if some stays on the surface, that's fine, too).

7. Place the pie shell on a rimmed baking sheet. Bake in the center of the oven for 60 to 70 minutes, or until the crust is deep golden brown. Place the baking sheet and pie on a wire rack to cool to room temperature. Serve drizzled with the caramel sauce.

I Can't Have an Affair Because It's Wrong (and I Don't Want Earl to Kill Me) Marbled Chocolate Cheesecake Pie

MAKES ONE 9½-INCH PIE

Here's one of those things you know in your heart you shouldn't do. I mean, just look at this thing: velvety white chocolate cheesecake with ripples of devilishly dark chocolate swirled right in. It tastes like sin, like the kind of satisfaction you maybe haven't felt in way, way too long. If this pie doesn't do you in, it might just save your life. At the very least you'll go out with a big old smile on your face.

chocolate cookie crumb pie shell

1¾ cups chocolate wafer cookie crumbs (about 36 cookies)

6 tablespoons (¾ stick) unsalted butter, melted

filling

4 ounces bittersweet chocolate, chopped

¾ cup heavy cream

4 ounces white chocolate, chopped

1½ (8-ounce) packages cream cheese, at room temperature

⅓ cup sweetened condensed milk

1½ teaspoons pure vanilla extract

1. **For the pie shell:** Preheat the oven to 350°F. Toss together the crumbs and butter in a medium bowl to moisten. Press the mixture onto the bottom and up the sides of a 9½-inch deep-dish pie pan. Refrigerate for at least 15 minutes to firm up the butter. Bake in the center of the oven for about 10 minutes, or until just set and fragrant. Place on a wire rack to cool to room temperature.

2. **For the filling:** Place the chopped chocolate in a medium heatproof bowl. Warm ¼ cup of the cream in a small saucepan over medium heat until small bubbles form around the edge. Pour over

recipe continues

the chocolate and let stand for 1 minute to soften, then whisk until smooth.

3. Melt the white chocolate in a large glass bowl in the microwave at 50 percent power in 20-second increments until the pieces begin to lose their shape, and then stir until smooth. Let stand to cool to room temperature.

4. Add the remaining ½ cup cream, the cream cheese, sweetened condensed milk, and vanilla. Beat with a mixer on high speed until smooth. Pour into the pie shell.

5. Pour the chocolate mixture over the cream cheese mixture and then swirl slowly with the end of a spoon to marble the filling. Refrigerate for 4 hours, or until firm.

A CHOP OFF THE OLD BLOCK

When a recipe calls for chopped chocolate, using chocolate chips or morsels might sound like a timesaver, but it's not the best choice. Chips and molded pieces usually contain paraffin and other ingredients that help them hold their shape, which are ingredients not found in pure chocolate.

Place the block of chocolate on a sturdy cutting board (covered with a sheet of parchment paper for easy cleanup, if you like). Starting on a corner, use a large, heavy knife, such as a chef's knife, to shave or break the block into small, even pieces no larger than ½ inch. Chocolate melts best when the pieces are of similar size. Don't try to chop a large block of chocolate in a food processor because it might damage or break the blade.

Another option for melted chocolate is to purchase nickel-size buttons of baking chocolate, often called pastilles. They are an ideal size for melting and don't require chopping.

PART FOUR

A Soft Place to Land: Custard and Cream Pies

THERE'RE ALL KINDS OF PIES IN THE WORLD, AND I'D BE HARD-pressed to pick one kind over the others. How do you choose among your own family? Some people like a pie busting out with luscious fruit like a cherry pie, and others favor something warm and soothing like a supper pie. But if I was forced to choose just one kind to put on the diner menu, I'd choose custard pie.

A custard pie is unbeatably satiny and decadent, like sneaking out and treating yourself to a spa day. It's a celebration of self-indulgent bliss. Custard needs a little more care while baking, but it's well worth the effort.

The main thing about a custard pie is you want it to be as creamy and light as you can get it, so you have to be careful not to overcook it, especially your baked custard pies such as Where There's a Whisk, There's a Way (page 120) and Razzleberry Buttermilk Custard Pie (page 108). The custard will firm up as it cools, so take it out of the oven when it can still jiggle a little bit right in the center.

Meringue is the lightest and fluffiest texture in these pies, which means taking special care when you whip it up. Meringue won't get those firm peaks if there's even a hint of grease or yolk in your mixing bowl. Make sure everything is clean, and separate your eggs carefully so you don't beat up those whites for nothing.

With cream pies, the base is usually so sweet and mellow that you'll want something with a tart edge to balance it out. A citrus flavor like the key limes in The Key (Lime) to Happiness Pie (page 117) or the lemon juice in Lulu's Lemonade Pies (page 102) works perfectly. Other times, it's nice to just fall into the dreamy soft sweetness, like Old Joe's Slice of Heaven Pie (page 114).

Point is, custard and cream pies put you in control of your life. You can go with the tart edge or make it soft and sweet. Most of these recipes won't even require a special trip to the market, long as you've got a few things like sugar, flour, butter, and eggs in your kitchen. And by now, of all the ingredients in the world, I bet you'll never let yourself run low on those.

~

LULU'S LEMONADE PIES
Like cups of pink lemonade, only tastier.

AREN'T YOU SWEET SWEET POTATO PIE
*A holiday classic, velvety with a touch
of caramel and maple syrup.*

RAZZLEBERRY BUTTERMILK CUSTARD PIE
*Rich buttermilk custard with a sharp taste of raspberry vinegar
that sparkles right through it.*

BANANA CREAM DAYDREAM PIE
Rich topping, soft banana custard, and filled with crunchy toffee pieces.

OLD JOE'S SLICE OF HEAVEN PIE
A classic coconut cream pie with a vanilla wafer crust.

THE KEY (LIME) TO HAPPINESS PIE
The closest thing there is to a margarita on a fork.

WHERE THERE'S A WHISK, THERE'S A WAY
An icebox wonder topped with a mile-high meringue.

WAKE UP AND SMELL THE COFFEE PIE
*A light and billowy chiffon, like the top of a cappuccino
finished with Kahlùa whipped cream.*

I DON'T WANT EARL'S BABY VINEGAR PIE
Like a Sour Patch Kid candy, where the puckering is half the fun.

~

Lulu's Lemonade Pies

~

These pies are like cups of pink lemonade, only tastier and you eat them with a fork. The filling is rich like a custard, and you can top them with candy or anything you want to make them even more special. These pies take me back to those endless summer days, running free with no place in particular to go. I named these for my daughter and I think you'll see they're perfect for that person in your life who deserves a little something tasty and pretty now and then.

Dough for a classic double-crust pie shell (page 17)

filling

1¼ cups sugar

2 tablespoons cornstarch

¼ teaspoon kosher salt

4 tablespoons (½ stick) unsalted butter, melted

¼ cup honey, plus more for drizzling

4 large eggs

½ cup half-and-half, at room temperature

¼ cup fresh lemon juice

1 to 3 drops red food coloring (optional)

sweetened whipped cream

1 cup heavy cream, chilled

¼ cup confectioners' sugar

1 teaspoon vanilla extract

Pink jelly beans, for decoration (optional)

---

1. **For the pie shells:** Divide the dough into eight equal balls. Roll each ball out to a 5-inch round and fit it into a mini-pie pan with a 4-ounce capacity. Fold under the edge of the pastry and crimp with a fork. Chill for at least 1 hour, or until firm.

2. Preheat the oven to 350°F. Line each pie shell with a sheet of aluminum foil, making sure the foil covers the crimped edge, and fill with ½ inch of pie weights or dried beans. Place on a rimmed baking sheet and bake in the upper third of the oven for 10 minutes. Lift up the corners of the foil, lift out the foil and weights, and bake for 10 minutes more, or until the crusts are dry and pale golden. Place the baking sheet and pie shells on a wire rack to cool to room temperature.

3. Reduce the oven temperature to 325°F.

4. **For the filling:** Whisk together the sugar, cornstarch, and salt in a large bowl.

recipe continues

MY HANDS PLUCK THE THINGS
I KNOW THAT I'LL NEED

I'LL TAKE THE SUGAR AND
BUTTER FROM THE PANTRY

I ADD THE FLOUR TO BEGIN
WHAT I'M HOPING TO START

AND THEN IT'S DOWN WITH
THE RECIPE AND BAKE FROM
THE HEART

Whisk in the melted butter. Whisk in the honey. (The mixture will be quite thick.) Whisk in the eggs. Whisk in the half-and-half and lemon juice. Whisk in the food coloring, 1 drop at a time, to tint the filling pink, if desired. Divide among the pie shells.

5. Bake in the center of the oven for 30 minutes, or until the filling is set. Place the baking sheet and pie shells on a wire rack to cool to room temperature.

6. **For the topping:** Beat the cream, confectioners' sugar, and vanilla to firm peaks in a chilled medium bowl with a mixer on high speed.

7. To serve, dollop or pipe the whipped cream onto each mini-pie and decorate with the jelly beans, if using.

DON'T LOSE YOUR COOL

Remember to keep your pastry dough cold! It's fine to stop at any point and return the mixture to the refrigerator to chill before beginning again. In hot weather, some bakers go so far as to chill their mixing bowl and utensils.

Aren't You Sweet Sweet Potato Pie

~

MAKES ONE 9½-INCH PIE

You can see straightaway that a gnarly sweet potato isn't for eating out of hand. And yet just as soon as you set it to roasting, suddenly the whole house smells of rich, deep, earthy sweetness. It's a holiday classic, velvety with a touch of caramel, even more so when you pair it with plenty of maple syrup. Add some fluffy whipped topping to dress it up for a grand look. A sweet potato isn't as pretty on the outside as, say, an apple, but once you put it in a pie you realize there's nothing sweeter on this earth. Which is what they'll be saying about you as soon as you serve up a slice of this.

Dough for classic double-crust pie (page 17)

egg wash

1 large egg

2 tablespoons water

filling

½ cup packed dark brown sugar

¼ teaspoon ground cinnamon

⅛ teaspoon ground allspice

⅛ teaspoon kosher salt

3 large eggs

¾ cup pure maple syrup, preferably Grade B

1½ cups sweet potato puree (page 107)

¾ cup half-and-half

maple whipped cream

1 cup heavy cream, chilled

2 tablespoons pure maple syrup

½ teaspoon pure vanilla extract

1. Preheat the oven to 350°F. Roll out one portion of the pie dough and line a 9½-inch pie pan. Refrigerate. Combine the egg and water to make an egg wash. Roll out the additional pastry and use a sharp knife or cookie cutters to create small shapes to decorate the top of the pie. Let them rest in the refrigerator to firm up for 15 minutes or so. Apply the cutouts around the edge of the pastry shell, reserving a few to top the pie, using a bit of egg wash to hold them in place. Blind bake as directed on page 20.

recipe continues

2. Reduce the oven temperature to 325°F.

3. Whisk together the brown sugar, cinnamon, allspice, and salt in a small bowl, making sure there are no lumps in the sugar.

4. Whisk the eggs in a large bowl until the whites and yolks are well combined. Whisk in the maple syrup. Whisk in the sweet potato puree. Whisk in the half-and-half. Whisk in the brown sugar mixture until well combined and smooth. Pour into the pie shell.

5. Bake the pie in the center of the oven for 1 hour, or until the filling is nearly set in the center and slightly puffed. When gently shaken, the center should jiggle slightly but no longer slosh or ripple, and a toothpick inserted 3 inches from the center should come out clean. The center of the pie will firm up as it cools. Place the reserved pastry cutouts on a baking sheet and brush them with egg wash. Bake them alongside the pie, taking them out after 20 minutes or when they look brown and dry. Arrange atop the pie filling.

6. **For the topping:** Combine the cream, maple syrup, and vanilla in a chilled medium bowl. With a mixer, beat on high speed until it holds firm peaks. Serve alongside the pie.

SMOOTH OPERATOR

Whether you boil or roast the sweet potatoes, cook them whole and peel them when cool enough to handle. Pass the warm potato flesh through a food mill or mash as smooth as possible with a handheld masher. Do not process, blend, or beat the potatoes, as this will cause them to become gluey. The puree should have the texture of canned pumpkin puree, so if it's too watery, drain in a fine-mesh sieve until firm enough to hold its shape on a spoon. Small, slender sweet potatoes (6 to 8 ounces each) tend to be less watery and fibrous.

Razzleberry Buttermilk Custard Pie

~

MAKES ONE 9½-INCH PIE

When I was a girl and my mama and I used to bake together, we didn't always have a lot, but you don't need a lot to make this pie. The rich buttermilk custard is tender and jiggly, with a sharp taste of raspberry vinegar that sparkles right through it. You get another dose of buttermilk tang in the crust and then again in the topping. If you want to get fancy about it, top it off with fresh raspberries, but believe me, this pie dazzles even without them.

Be sure you use fresh, whole buttermilk. Milk that's curdled with vinegar or lemon juice might add some sourness, but nothing can replace the tangy flavor and delicate texture you get from buttermilk. It makes a world of difference.

buttermilk pie shell

1¼ cups unbleached all-purpose flour

1 tablespoon sugar

½ teaspoon kosher salt

4 tablespoons (½ stick) unsalted butter, cut into small cubes and chilled

¼ cup vegetable shortening, cut into bits and chilled

3 to 4 tablespoons well-shaken buttermilk, chilled

filling

2 large eggs, separated

6 tablespoons (¾ stick) unsalted butter, at room temperature

1 cup granulated sugar

3 tablespoons unbleached all-purpose flour

2 tablespoons raspberry vinegar

½ teaspoon pure vanilla extract

¼ teaspoon kosher salt

1 cup well-shaken buttermilk, at room temperature

buttermilk whipped cream topping

½ cup heavy cream, chilled

½ cup well-shaken buttermilk, chilled

2 tablespoons confectioners' sugar

3 cups fresh red, yellow, and/or black raspberries

Confectioners' sugar, for dusting

1. **For the pie shell:** Whisk together the flour, sugar, and salt in a large bowl. Work in the butter and shortening with a pastry blender (or pulse in the bowl of a food processor) until the mixture is crumbly with a few pieces of butter the size of small peas. Stir in 3 tablespoons of the buttermilk with a fork (or pulse in the

recipe continues

bowl of a food processor) to form large clumps that pull in all the dry ingredients. Squeeze a small pinch of dough; if it is too dry to hold together, stir in more buttermilk, 1 teaspoon at a time. Pour onto a piece of plastic wrap. Gather and form into a ball, then flatten into a disk about ¾ inch thick. Wrap well and chill at least 30 minutes.

2. Roll the dough on a lightly floured surface to a 12-inch round. Fit it into a 9½-inch pie pan with about a ½-inch overhang. Turn under and crimp the edge. Refrigerate until chilled and firm, at least 30 minutes.

3. Preheat the oven to 350°F. Place the pie pan on a rimmed baking sheet. Line the pie shell with aluminum foil and fill with ½ inch of pie weights or dried beans. Bake in the upper third of the oven for 15 minutes. Fold up the corners of the foil, lift out the foil and weights, and continue baking for 10 minutes more, or until the pie shell looks dry and is pale golden. Place the baking sheet and pie shell on a wire rack to cool to room temperature. Leave the oven on.

4. **For the filling:** Beat the egg whites in a large, very clean glass or metal bowl with a mixer on low speed until the whites are frothy. Increase to high speed and beat to soft peaks.

5. Beat the butter and sugar until light and fluffy in a large bowl with the mixer on high speed. Beat in the egg yolks. Beat in the flour, vinegar, vanilla, and salt. With the mixer on low speed, add the buttermilk in a slow, steady stream. Don't worry if the mixture looks a bit curdled at this point!

6. Use a spatula to fold about one-third of the whites into the egg yolk mixture to lighten the batter. Fold in the rest of the whites. (It is better to have a few visible wisps of whites than to stir so thoroughly that you deflate them.)

7. Pour the filling into the pie shell, still on the baking sheet. Bake in the center of the oven for 45 minutes, or until the filling is lightly browned. When gently shaken, the center should jiggle slightly but no longer slosh or ripple, and a toothpick inserted 3 inches from the center should come out clean. The center of the pie will firm up as it cools. Place on a wire rack to cool to room temperature.

8. **For the topping:** Beat the cream, buttermilk, and confectioners' sugar to firm peaks in a chilled medium bowl with a mixer on high speed. Spread over the pie and smooth the top. Cover the top of the pie with the raspberries. Dust with confectioners' sugar. Serve at room temperature or lightly chilled.

Banana Cream Daydream Pie

MAKES ONE 9½-INCH PIE

This pie's like a wonderful dream with a last-minute twist. You start with the rich topping. Next your tongue floats around in the soft banana custard. Then, just when you think everything's gone all soft and sweet, you find the crunchy toffee pieces at the bottom. Surprise!

This is a wonderful pie for company or for children. Best thing is, it's not a dream—it's the real thing.

filling

¾ cup sugar

⅓ cup unbleached all-purpose flour

¼ teaspoon kosher salt

3 large egg yolks

2½ cups whole milk

2 tablespoons unsalted butter, chilled

1 teaspoon pure vanilla extract

½ cup toffee baking bits

2 medium bananas (see note on page 113)

9½-inch blind-baked pie shell (page 20), cooled to room temperature

topping

1 cup heavy cream

3 tablespoons confectioners' sugar

1 medium banana

1 teaspoon fresh lemon juice (optional)

1. **For the filling:** Whisk together the sugar, flour, and salt in medium bowl. Whisk the eggs yolks in a large bowl.

2. Heat the milk in a large saucepan over medium heat until it bubbles around the edge. Whisking continuously, add the milk to the sugar mixture in a slow, steady stream and whisk until smooth. Pour back into the saucepan and cook, stirring continuously with a heatproof spatula, for 2 to 3 minutes, or until thick enough to coat the back of the spatula.

3. Whisking continuously, add about ½ cup of the hot milk mixture to the egg yolks to temper them. Pour the eggs into the saucepan and cook, stirring continuously with the spatula, for 5 minutes, or until the custard comes to a boil and thickly

recipe continues

coats the back of the spatula. Remove the pan from the heat, add the butter, and stir until melted. Stir in the vanilla.

4. Sprinkle the toffee bits in the pie shell. Slice the bananas into ¼-inch-thick rounds and place in the pie shell. Pour the warm custard mixture over the bananas. Chill until cold and firm.

5. **For the topping:** Combine the cream and confectioners' sugar in a large bowl and beat with a mixer until stiff peaks form. Slice the banana ¼ inch thick and brush the slices with the lemon juice to keep the slices from browning if you will not be serving immediately. Pipe or spread the whipped cream onto the pie and top with the banana slices.

NOTE: *Ripe, firm bananas that are yellow from top to bottom and lightly covered in brown freckles are the best choice for the filling.*

Old Joe's Slice of Heaven Pie

This pie was one of my biggest hits at the diner: a classic coconut cream pie, except I added a vanilla wafer crust to take it even higher. More heavenly maybe, if you imagine heaven as the perfect harmony of soft and crunchy. The coconut gives texture to the light, soft cream, so you're all ready for the sweet bite of the crust when it comes. I don't know much about heaven, but I do know about baking, and this is a match made in you-know-where.

pie shell

1¾ cups vanilla wafer crumbs

6 tablespoons (¾ stick) unsalted butter, melted

filling

½ cup granulated sugar

2 large eggs

1 large egg yolk

3 tablespoons unbleached all-purpose flour

1½ cups whole milk

1 tablespoon unsalted butter

1 teaspoon pure vanilla extract

¼ teaspoon coconut flavoring

3 cups sweetened flaked coconut

topping

1½ cups heavy cream

¼ cup confectioners' sugar

1. **For the pie shell:** Preheat the oven to 350°F. Toss together the crumbs and butter in a medium bowl to moisten. Press the mixture onto the bottom and up the sides of a 9½-inch deep-dish pie pan. Refrigerate for at least 15 minutes to firm up the butter. Bake in the center of the oven for about 10 minutes, or until just set and fragrant. Place on a wire rack to cool to room temperature.

2. **For the filling:** Whisk the granulated sugar, eggs, egg yolk, and flour in a medium bowl. Bring the milk to a simmer in a medium saucepan over medium heat. Whisking continuously, add the hot milk to the egg mixture in a slow, steady stream and whisk until smooth. Pour into the saucepan and cook, stirring

recipe continues

continuously with a heatproof spatula, for 5 minutes, or until the mixture comes to a boil and thickens. Remove the pan from the heat, drop in the butter, and stir until melted. Stir in the vanilla and coconut flavoring.

3. Pass the filling through a fine-mesh sieve into a clean bowl, using a rubber spatula to press it through the mesh. Stir in 1½ cups of the coconut. Press a piece of buttered parchment paper directly onto the surface to prevent a skin from forming. Let cool to room temperature, then refrigerate for at least 1 hour, or until chilled. Pour the filling into the cooled pie shell.

4. **For the topping:** In a large bowl using a mixer, beat the cream with the confectioners' sugar until stiff peaks form. Pile the whipped cream onto the filling, mounding it in the center, and sprinkle with the remaining 1½ cups of coconut. Refrigerate until set.

The Key (Lime) to Happiness Pie

MAKES ONE 9½-INCH PIE

Real happiness never tastes how you thought it would. A lime is about the sourest, unfriendliest excuse for a fruit you could ever hope to meet. But sweet-talk it with condensed milk and soothe it with egg yolks, and it's pure delight. A little tequila and triple sec—well, I'm not saying they're the key to happiness, but they can't hurt, either. And for the final touch, the note of salt in the pretzel crust and the whipped cream topping make this pie the closest thing there is to a margarita on a fork. Serve it very well chilled.

pretzel crumb pie shell

1¾ cups pretzel crumbs

2 tablespoons granulated sugar

6 tablespoons (¾ stick) unsalted butter, melted

filling

2 (14-ounce) cans sweetened condensed milk

4 large egg yolks

¾ cup bottled key lime juice, preferably Nellie and Joe's brand

¼ cup blanco tequila

1 tablespoon triple sec

salted whipped cream topping

1 cup heavy cream, chilled

2 tablespoons confectioners' sugar

1 teaspoon pure vanilla extract

1½ teaspoons coarse or flaked sea salt

Grated lemon zest

1. **For the pie shell:** Preheat the oven to 350°F. Toss together the crumbs, sugar, and butter in a medium bowl to moisten. Press the mixture onto the bottom and up the sides of a 9½-inch deep-dish pie pan. Refrigerate for at least 15 minutes to firm up the butter. Bake in the center of the oven for about 10 minutes, or until just set and fragrant. Place on a wire rack to cool to room temperature.

2. **For the filling:** Whisk together the condensed milk and egg yolks in a large bowl until smooth. Add the key lime juice, tequila, and triple sec and whisk until smooth. Let stand for 5 minutes to thicken. Pour into the pie shell.

3. Bake in the center of the oven for 15 minutes. Place on a wire rack to cool

recipe continues

to room temperature. Refrigerate for 1 hour, or until chilled.

4. **For the topping:** Use a mixer to beat the cream, confectioners' sugar, and vanilla to firm peaks on high speed. Transfer the cream to a piping bag fitted with a rippled tip (#885) and pipe onto the pie decoratively. (You can also just pile the whipped cream directly onto the pie and spread with an offset spatula if you prefer.) Sprinkle with the salt and lemon zest before serving.

THE KEY TO LIMES

Key limes are smaller and rounder than conventional limes, and can be hard to come by in many areas of the country. Although in most cases fresh fruit juice makes for a tastier pie, unless you have access to very fresh, juicy key limes, this pie works best when made with bottled key lime juice, which delivers consistent acidity and flavor.

Where There's a Whisk, There's a Way

MAKES ONE 9½-INCH PIE

When life gives me lemons, I bake them up in a pie. The gentle zip of Meyer lemons in this icebox wonder, with a mile-high meringue, brings brightness and balances out the fluffy, sugary topping. But what if the lemons life brings you aren't Meyer lemons? Don't worry: just use half regular lemon, half tangerine for the zest and the juice. It'll be just as amazing. In baking, as in life, there's always more than one way to make lemonade.

meyer lemon cookie pie shell

1¾ cups crisp Meyer lemon cookie crumbs

6 tablespoons (¾ stick) unsalted butter, melted

filling

4 large egg yolks

1 (14-ounce) can sweetened condensed milk

4 teaspoons lightly packed finely grated fresh Meyer lemon zest

½ cup fresh Meyer lemon juice

meringue topping

6 large egg whites, at room temperature

½ teaspoon cream of tartar

½ teaspoon pure vanilla extract

¾ cup sugar

1. **For the pie shell:** Preheat the oven to 350°F.

2. Toss together the crumbs and butter in a medium bowl to moisten. Press the mixture onto the bottom and up the sides of a 9½-inch deep-dish pie pan. Refrigerate for at least 15 minutes to firm up the butter. Bake in the center of the oven for about 10 minutes, or until just set and fragrant. Place on a wire rack to cool to room temperature. Keep the oven on.

3. **For the filling:** Whisk together the egg yolks and condensed milk in a large bowl. Add the lemon zest and lemon juice and whisk until smooth. Pour the filling into the pie shell. Bake in the center of the oven for 15 minutes, or until set. Meanwhile, make the meringue.

recipe continues

A DREAM NEEDS BELIEVING
TO TASTE LIKE THE REAL THING . . .

4. **For the meringue:** Beat the egg whites, cream of tartar, and vanilla in a large glass or metal bowl with a mixer on medium speed until the whites are cloudy. Increase to high speed and beat the whites to soft peaks. Add the sugar 1 tablespoon at a time and beat to stiff peaks.

5. Spoon the meringue over the warm filling, spreading it to touch the crust and mounding it in the center. Make attractive swirls with the back of the spoon.

6. Bake for 30 minutes, or until the meringue is golden brown with slightly darker peaks. Place on a wire rack to cool to room temperature.

NOTE: *Meyer lemons are less tart than regular lemons, with a flavor that is often described as lemon mixed with mandarin orange. They are available in most grocery stores from May through December, but when Meyer lemons are unavailable, replace their juice and zest with equal parts tangerine and regular lemon zest and juice.*

Crisp Meyer lemon cookies are easy to find in most grocery stores, but vanilla wafers or shortbread cookies make a fine substitution.

PEAK PERFORMANCE

Fluffy meringue, piled high and baked just until starting to brown on the tips of each swirled drift, is a signature of a great diner pie. To whip up the loftiest meringue, start with a very clean and dry metal or glass bowl. Some bakers even take the extra step of sloshing a splash of vinegar and a pinch of salt around in the bowl to remove every trace of grease or errant fingerprints; if you do this, just pour out the vinegar and salt without rinsing the bowl. Next, be sure there isn't even a speck of egg yolk or shell in the whites. Add a bit of cream of tartar to stabilize the whites so they hold their shape. And when you top your pie, be sure to spread the meringue all the way to the edge of the crust, covering the filling completely.

Wake Up and Smell the Coffee Pie

MAKES ONE 9½-INCH PIE

This one'll give you extra reason to get out of bed in the morning. The chiffon is light and billowy, like the top of a cappuccino. The Kahlùa whipped cream makes it even more deluxe. It's a pampering, full-on decadent way to jump-start a workday. It gets you ready for hustling out to a long day of taking orders and serving customers and . . . On second thought—maybe this pie's a perfect reason to eat breakfast in bed this morning. I'm sure you can think up an excuse for skipping work with all that pep you got now.

graham cracker pie shell

1³/4 cups graham cracker crumbs (about 16 sheets of crackers)

6 tablespoons (³/4 stick) unsalted butter, melted

chiffon filling

1/4 cup water

1 (.25-ounce) envelope unflavored gelatin

4 large egg yolks, beaten

1/2 teaspoon kosher salt

1 cup sugar

1/2 cup brewed espresso, at room temperature

4 large egg whites

kahlùa whipped cream topping

1 cup heavy cream, chilled

2 tablespoons Kahlùa or other coffee liqueur

Handful of chocolate-covered espresso beans, for garnish

1. **For the pie shell:** Preheat the oven to 350°F. Toss together the crumbs and butter in a medium bowl to moisten. Press the mixture onto the bottom and up the sides of a 9½-inch pie pan. Refrigerate for at least 15 minutes to firm up the butter. Bake in the center of the oven for about 10 minutes, or until just set and fragrant. Place on a wire rack to cool to room temperature.

2. **For the filling:** Place the water in a small bowl and sprinkle with the gelatin; let stand for 5 minutes to soften.

3. Whisk together the egg yolks, salt, ³/4 cup of the sugar, and the espresso until smooth in a medium saucepan. Cook over medium heat for about 3 minutes, stirring with a heatproof spatula, or until

recipe continues

the mixture thickens enough to coat the back of the spatula. Stir in the softened gelatin. Transfer to a bowl and refrigerate for 15 minutes, or until the mixture thickens slightly.

4. Beat the egg whites until frothy in a clean glass or metal bowl with a mixer on low speed. Increase to high speed and beat to soft peaks. Gradually add the remaining ¼ cup of sugar and beat to stiff peaks. Fold into the espresso mixture. Spoon into the cooled pie shell and refrigerate 3 hours, or until firm.

5. **For the topping:** Beat the cream and Kahlùa to firm peaks in a chilled medium bowl with a mixer on high speed. Spread over the chilled pie. Decorate with the chocolate-covered espresso beans.

DON'T BE CLINGY

When cooking a cream filling or custard that contains egg yolks, press the yolks through a fine-mesh sieve into a small bowl, using a rubber spatula to press them through the mesh, leaving behind any egg white clinging to the yolks. This step reduces the chance that the filling will curdle.

I Don't Want Earl's Baby Vinegar Pie

When life gets sour, baking's what always lifts me back up. One of the most useful things I've learned in a lifetime of baking pies is that, as nice as sweet can be, sometimes sour makes things interesting.

Like this pie. Vinegar's not something you generally think of for a dessert, but the vinegar in this pie gives the custard just the right amount of tart to cut through the sugar. The sweet and sour flavors set each other off wonderfully, and the pastry shell adds a gentle crunch. It's like a Sour Patch Kid candy, where the puckering is half the fun. Next time you want to bake but the cupboard is bare, I bet you'll find what you need to make this pie way in the back, and turn that sour situation right around.

filling

3 large egg yolks, lightly beaten

1 cup sugar

1 cup cornstarch

¼ teaspoon kosher salt

1¾ cups boiling water

¼ cup apple cider vinegar

¼ teaspoon balsamic vinegar

2 tablespoons coarse sugar, such as Demerara

9½-inch blind-baked pie shell (page 20), cooled to room temperature

1. **For the filling:** Set up a double boiler or place a metal bowl over a saucepan and bring the water in the bottom pan to a simmer. Whisk together the egg yolks, sugar, cornstarch, and salt and place over the simmering water. Whisking continuously, add the boiling water in a slow, steady stream. Whisk in the apple cider vinegar. Cook for 12 minutes, or until thick and smooth. Remove the bowl from the heat and whisk in the balsamic vinegar.

2. Pour the warm filling into the cooled pie shell. Press a piece of buttered parchment paper directly onto the surface to prevent a skin from forming. Let cool to room temperature and then refrigerate at least 1 hour, or until set and chilled. Just before serving, sprinkle the filling with the coarse sugar.

PART FIVE

Lulus:
Blue-Ribbon Winners

MY MAMA USED TO SAY YOU CAN LIVE TO BE ONE HUNDRED IF YOU give up all the things that make you wanna live to be one hundred, and all the pies in this section fit that description—they're real lulus! These are pies that send a message, whether you want to impress, to score points, or to celebrate good news. They may take a little more time and effort, but you can be sure those little extra steps are gonna pay off in the end.

When you make a lulu, you want to go a little bit beyond over the top to full-blown showstopper. Imagine you're entering a pie contest and you want to come up with something that will make those judges sit up and take notice. Start by adding a little something extra to your crust, like a pinch of chile or the crunch of a macadamia nut cookie. Layer on your fillings one, two, even three at a time. If there's a secret hidden flavor in there to tickle the taste buds, so much the better. And don't hold back on the toppings; shower down a blizzard of bacon streusel or crush up some extra cookie bits to add crunch and contrast. Top it all off with marshmallows, a moonpie, or some pretty piped flavored whipped cream and sprinkles. Bake a cake on top of your pie and flip the whole magilla onto a cake plate for twice the fun and twice the delicious-ness. Or pile one pie atop the other for a super holiday stack pie. In other words, once you get inspired, don't stop until you've put everything you've got into that creation.

And sure, these pies are rich. But like my mama always told me, it only takes a taste when you know it's good. Sometimes one bite is more than enough to let you know you want more of the thing you just got a taste of.

~

DEEP-DISH BLUEBERRY-BACON PIE
Like a perfect diner breakfast all cozied up in a slice of pie.

PINEAPPLE UPSIDE-DOWN PIE
It's a fruit tart in a cake, and it's a cake in a pie shell.

MEET YOUR DREAM CHOCOLATE CREAM PIE
*Chocolate filling mixed with intense passion fruit
and an electric tingle of chile.*

LIFE'S A ROCKY ROAD MACADAMIA MOUSSE PIES
*White chocolate chips, crunchy macadamia nuts,
and a creamy white chocolate mousse.*

LOVE, LIBERTY, AND THE PURSUIT OF HAPPINESS PIE
This stack pie is proof in red, white, and blue that some pies are happier united.

JUMPING WITHOUT A NET BOTTOMLESS
STRAWBERRY-RHUBARB CUPS
Topped with billowy meringue and drizzled with strawberry-rhubarb syrup.

MERMAID MARSHMALLOW PIE
*Like an old-time ambrosia salad—sweet, but
with a fun tartness from the oranges.*

GETTING OUT OF THE MUD FROZEN MUD PIE
*Cool, sweet ice cream in a crushed sugar cone shell
and glazed with thick, fudgy chocolate.*

THANKS FOR TAKING ME TO THE MOON
PEANUT BUTTER MOONPIE PIE
*Peanut butter cream topped with
marshmallow whipped cream and MoonPies.*

~

Deep-Dish Blueberry-Bacon Pie

MAKES ONE 9½-INCH PIE

Did you ever dip your bacon into the puddle of maple syrup around your stack of blueberry pancakes? That's what got me to thinking about this recipe. It's like a perfect diner breakfast—blueberry pancakes, syrup, oatmeal, and bacon—all cozied up in a slice of pie. The salty bacon brings out the best flavors in the blueberries and the sugar syrup. I can't decide if it's breakfast dressed up as dessert or the other way around, but I guarantee it's simpler and more delicious than either one.

Easy as pie.

pie shell

1¾ cups gingersnap cookie crumbs (about 30 cookies)

6 tablespoons (¾ stick) unsalted butter, melted

bacon streusel

3 ounces smoked bacon, chilled and cut crosswise into ¼-inch-wide pieces

½ cup old-fashioned rolled oats

½ cup maple sugar or packed light brown sugar

¼ cup unbleached all-purpose flour

½ teaspoon ground cinnamon

½ teaspoon ground cardamom

4 tablespoons (½ stick) unsalted butter, cut into cubes and chilled

¼ cup pecan pieces

2 tablespoons finely chopped crystallized ginger

filling

⅔ cup granulated sugar

¼ cup cornstarch

1 teaspoon finely grated lemon zest

5 cups fresh blueberries

2 tablespoons fresh lemon juice

1. **For the pie shell:** Preheat the oven to 350°F. Toss together the crumbs and butter in a medium bowl to moisten. Press the mixture onto the bottom and up the sides of a 9½-inch deep-dish pie pan. Refrigerate for at least 15 minutes to firm up the butter. Bake in the center of the oven for about 10 minutes, or until just set and fragrant. Let cool to room temperature on a wire rack.

recipe continues

Guest C

TABLE NO.   PERSONS   SERVER NO.

BEV • APPET • SOUP/SALAD • ENTREE

1 DEEP DISH
BLUEBERRY
BACON PIE

—18

2. **For the streusel:** Cook the bacon in a large skillet over medium heat for 20 minutes, or until rendered and crisp, stirring often. Use a slotted spoon to transfer to paper towels to drain and cool.

3. Stir together the oats, maple sugar, flour, cinnamon, and cardamom in a medium bowl. Work in the butter with your fingertips or a pastry blender until the mixture is crumbly. Fold in the cooled bacon, pecans, and ginger. Pinch about one-third of the mixture into balls the size of marbles; leave the rest crumbly. Cover and refrigerate for at least 30 minutes, or until the butter is firm.

4. **For the filling:** Stir together the granulated sugar, cornstarch, and lemon zest in a large bowl. Add the blueberries and lemon juice and toss to coat. Let stand for 30 minutes, stirring occasionally.

5. Preheat the oven to 375°F. Place the pie shell on a rimmed baking sheet. Pour the filling into the shell. Arrange the streusel over the filling. Bake in the center of the oven for 60 to 70 minutes, or until the streusel is deep golden brown and the filling is bubbling. Cover the pie with a flat sheet of aluminum foil after the first 20 minutes to prevent overbrowning. Let cool to room temperature on a wire rack.

Pineapple Upside-Down Pie

MAKES ONE 9-INCH PIE

I always turn to pie when my life gets crazy. For those times when you can't figure out which end is up, an upside-down cake can make the world look right-side-up again.

Nothing in this world makes as much sense as sugar, butter, and flour, but this pie still surprises. It's a fruit tart in a cake, and it's a cake in a pie shell. The crust around the cake makes it like two desserts in one, with dripping golden bits of pineapple and soft sweet glazed cherries all over the top. Or is that the bottom?

filling

2 tablespoons unsalted butter

1/4 cup lightly packed brown sugar

4 slices canned pineapple: 3 cut in semicircles, 1 left whole

6 maraschino cherries, halved

3/4 cup unbleached all-purpose flour

1 teaspoon baking powder

Pinch of kosher salt

3 tablespoons vegetable shortening

1/3 cup granulated sugar

1 large egg

1/3 cup whole milk

1/2 teaspoon pure vanilla extract

Dough for a classic single-crust pie shell (page 17)

1. **For the filling:** Preheat the oven to 400°F. Place the butter in a shallow 9-inch pie pan and put the pan in the preheating oven to melt the butter, 5 to 7 minutes. A pie pan with at least a ½-inch lip edge works well, so there is room to crimp the crust edge onto the lip, creating more of a crust surrounding the edge when the pie is turned over.

2. Sprinkle the brown sugar evenly over the melted butter. Place the whole pineapple slice in the center of the pan and arrange the half slices around it. Fill in the gaps with cherry halves, cut side down. Set aside.

3. To assemble the cake batter, sift together the flour, baking powder, and salt in a medium bowl. In another bowl whisk the vegetable shortening and granulated sugar together until light and fluffy. Add the egg, milk, and vanilla and whisk until incorporated. Add the dry ingredients to the batter slowly, whisking just until combined.

recipe continues

4. Pour the batter into the pie pan, being careful not to dislodge the fruit. Smooth the top of the batter.

5. **For the crust:** Roll out the pie crust and carefully lay it over the cake batter. Crimp the edges, creating a seal around the edge of the pie pan and fully enclosing the cake batter.

6. Bake for 10 minutes, then reduce the heat to 350°F and bake for 20 to 25 minutes longer, or until a toothpick inserted into the middle of the cake (through the crust) comes out clean.

7. Immediately place a large plate over the top of the pie, and carefully invert the plate and pie pan. Leave the pie pan in place for 10 minutes, then remove the pan slowly to reveal your Pineapple Upside-Down Pie! Let cool completely before slicing and serving.

GETTING A RISE

Baking powder and other leavening agents are shelf-stable but not everlasting. Replace them annually, or every 6 months if they've been stored in high heat and humidity. For best results, keep them in a cool, dry place such as a cabinet or pantry, away from the stove.

Meet Your Dream Chocolate Cream Pie

MAKES ONE 9½-INCH PIE

Give someone a piece of this pie and I guarantee the deal is sealed.

Here is a sexy treat for times when you know exactly what you want—and you want 'em to know you know. It's all innocence on the outside with a touch of danger beneath the surface. Chocolate's an irresistible delight all on its own, but you follow it up with the unmistakable intensity of passion fruit and an electric tingle of chile? Now you're talkin'. Top it with cream rosettes to keep the girlish illusion going so they'll never know what hit them.

---

spicy chocolate cookie pie shell

1¾ cups chocolate wafer cookie crumbs (about 36 cookies)

6 tablespoons (¾ stick) unsalted butter, melted

2 teaspoons ground ancho chile, or ground chipotle for more heat

¼ teaspoon cayenne pepper

filling

1 cup passion fruit jam or jelly

8 ounces bittersweet chocolate, chopped

⅔ cup granulated sugar

¼ cup cornstarch

½ teaspoon kosher salt

4 large egg yolks

3 cups whole milk

2 tablespoons unsalted butter, chilled

1 teaspoon pure vanilla extract

chocolate whipped cream topping

1 cup heavy cream, chilled

1 teaspoon pure vanilla extract

¼ cup confectioners' sugar

3 tablespoons unsweetened cocoa powder

---

1. **For the pie shell:** Preheat the oven to 350°F. Toss together the crumbs, butter, and spices in a medium bowl to moisten. Press the mixture onto the bottom and up the sides of a 9½-inch pie pan.

Refrigerate for at least 15 minutes to firm up the butter. Bake in the center of the oven for about 10 minutes, or until just set and fragrant. Place on a wire rack and let cool to room temperature.

recipe continues

2. **For the filling:** Spread the jam gently over the bottom of the pie shell.

3. Place the chocolate in a large glass or metal bowl.

4. Whisk together the sugar, cornstarch, salt, and egg yolks in a large, heavy saucepan. Whisking continuously, add the milk in a slow, steady stream. Bring to a boil over medium heat, stirring slowly with a heatproof spatula. Reduce the heat and simmer, stirring continuously, for 1 minute, or until the filling is very thick. Pass the hot pastry cream through a fine-mesh sieve into the bowl of chocolate, using a rubber spatula to press it through the mesh. Let stand for 1 minute to soften the chocolate, drop in the butter, and stir until smooth. Stir in the vanilla. Press a piece of buttered parchment paper directly onto the surface to prevent a skin from forming. Let cool to room temperature. Pour into the pie shell and refrigerate for at least 6 hours, or until set.

5. **For the topping:** Whisk together the cream, vanilla, confectioners' sugar, and cocoa powder in a large chilled bowl until the dry ingredients mix into the cream. Using a mixer, beat on high speed until it holds firm peaks. Scoop the whipped cream into a pastry bag fitted with a large star tip. Pipe rosettes onto the filling, spacing them as evenly as possible.

Life's a Rocky Road Macadamia Mousse Pies

~

MAKES 12 (4-OUNCE) PIES

These pies are pretty much cookies and milk kicked up a few degrees. The cookies have white chocolate chips and a soft crunch from the macadamia nuts, and the "milk" is a rich and creamy white chocolate mousse. When you put a pie in a jar, it can go anywhere, like a picnic or as a treat in a lunch box. You don't have to worry about dipping, and there's never spilled milk to cry over. A jar pie is the perfect after-school snack, even if school was a long, long time ago. You'll get a lot more cookies than you need for the jar pies from this recipe and you can freeze any extras if you want, but I'm guessing they won't hang around long enough.

white chocolate macadamia nut cookies

2¼ cups unbleached all-purpose flour

1 teaspoon baking soda

¼ teaspoon kosher salt

1 cup firmly packed light brown sugar

½ cup granulated sugar

1 cup (2 sticks) salted butter, at room temperature

2 large eggs

2 teaspoons pure vanilla extract

1 cup chopped macadamia nuts

12 ounces white chocolate chips

crust

10 White Chocolate Macadamia Nut Cookies, crushed

4 tablespoons (½ stick) unsalted butter, melted

filling

3 cups heavy cream, chilled

12 ounces white chocolate chips

1 teaspoon pure vanilla extract

¼ cup granulated sugar

⅔ cup chopped macadamia nuts

topping

¼ cup chopped macadamia nuts

1. Preheat the oven to 350°F.

2. **For the cookies:** Stir together the flour, baking soda, and salt in a bowl and set aside.

3. In a separate bowl using a mixer, blend the sugars on medium speed. Add the salted butter and beat until fluffy, scraping down the sides of the bowl

recipe continues

as needed. Add the eggs and vanilla and beat until fully combined. Add the dry ingredients, macadamia nuts, and white chocolate chips and mix just until combined.

4. Drop the batter by rounded spoonfuls onto ungreased baking sheets. Bake for 10 to 12 minutes. Transfer the cookies to wire racks to cool completely, leaving the oven on. (The cookies can also be made a day or two ahead of time and stored in an airtight container.) Set aside six to eight of the cookies for garnish.

5. **For the crust:** Crush ten of the cookies into crumbs. (You will have cookies left over for the cookie jar or to freeze.) Place the crushed cookies in the bowl of a food processor and whir until finely ground, about 20 seconds. Add the unsalted butter and pulse until the mixture begins to clump together. Divide the crumb mixture equally among twelve 4-ounce mason jars with lids, pressing it down into an even layer. Arrange the jars on a rimmed baking sheet and bake for 5 minutes. Let cool completely.

6. **For the filling:** While the crusts cool, bring 1 cup of the heavy cream to a simmer in a saucepan over medium heat. Place the white chocolate chips in a heatproof bowl and pour the hot cream and vanilla over the chips. Let stand for 2 minutes, then gently stir until smooth. Set aside to cool completely, about 30 minutes, stirring occasionally.

7. In a large bowl using a mixer, beat the remaining 2 cups of heavy cream on medium speed with the sugar until stiff peaks form, about 5 minutes. Gently stir 1 cup of the whipped cream into the cooled chocolate mixture, then fold in the remaining whipped cream. Fold in the macadamia nuts.

8. Spoon the mixture onto the cooled crusts, filling the jars almost to the top. Crumble the reserved six to eight white chocolate macadamia cookies and sprinkle them over the top of the filling.

9. **For the topping:** Divide the ¼ cup macadamia nuts evenly among the jars. Cover and chill for 6 to 12 hours. Store in the refrigerator until ready to serve.

Love, Liberty, and the Pursuit of Happiness Pie

MAKES ONE 9½-INCH DOUBLE-DECKER PIE

We hold this truth to be self-evident: you *can* live the dream. Or at least, you can bake the dream. This stack pie is proof in red, white, and blue that some pies are happier united. The tart snap of strawberries would be enough all on their own, and plenty of folks are fond of blueberry pie, but marry them up and together, they are a declaration of deliciousness. It's love and liberty on a fork, and we could all use a slice of that.

strawberry filling

1 quart fresh strawberries, hulled and sliced

1/3 cup sugar

1½ teaspoons fresh lemon juice

3 tablespoons water

1 (.25-ounce) envelope unflavored gelatin (2¼ teaspoons)

blueberry filling

1½ pints fresh blueberries

1/3 cup sugar

1½ teaspoons fresh lemon juice

1 (.25-ounce) envelope plain gelatin

Two 9½-inch blind-baked pie shells (page 20), cooled to room temperature

cream cheese topping

1 (8-ounce) package cream cheese, at room temperature

1 cup heavy cream

2 tablespoons confectioners' sugar

1 teaspoon pure vanilla extract

Red and blue sanding sugar or additional fresh fruit for garnish

1. **For the fillings:** Pulse enough of the strawberries in the bowl of a food processor to make 2 cups of chunky puree, reserving the remaining sliced berries. Pour into a bowl, stir in the sugar, and let stand for 30 minutes, stirring occasionally to dissolve the sugar. Stir in the lemon juice.

2. Pour the water into a small heatproof bowl. Sprinkle the gelatin over the water and let stand for 5 minutes. Heat the gelatin mixture in the microwave on high in 5-second increments until it is melted and hot. Stir well and then whisk into the strawberry mixture.

recipe continues

3. Repeat the process with the blueberries, reserving the remaining whole berries. Refrigerate the strawberry and blueberry fillings separately for about 30 minutes, or until the mixtures thicken to the consistency of corn syrup.

4. Stir the strawberry mixture well to loosen any gelatin that hardens on the edge and fold in the remaining sliced strawberries. Do the same for the blueberry mixture and fold in the remaining whole blueberries.

5. Refrigerate for 2 hours, or until each mixture reaches the consistency of thick preserves. Pour the strawberry filling into one cooled pie shell. Slip the second pie shell out of its pan and place on top of the strawberry filling, and then pour in the blueberry filling. Refrigerate at least 3 hours, or until the fillings are set.

6. **For the topping:** Beat the cream cheese until soft in a medium bowl with a mixer on medium speed. Add the cream, confectioners' sugar, and vanilla; increase to high speed and beat to firm peaks. Pile the cream cheese topping onto the pie. Garnish with colored sanding sugar or additional fresh fruit.

Jumping Without a Net
Bottomless Strawberry-Rhubarb Cups

~

SERVES 6

In baking it helps to know what you're doing ahead of time, but every once in a while you have to wing it. One day the diner was low on supplies, but we still needed a pie of the day. Well, I had a few stalks of rhubarb, so there's your tartness. I had sugar and strawberries for sweetness. What I didn't have that day was flour—I was fresh out.

No matter. I whipped up a billowy meringue for the tops and drizzled it with strawberry-rhubarb syrup. These are sweet pies, but the rhubarb keeps it all perfectly balanced. Like my mama used to say, a dream is a soft place to land. Sometimes it pays to take a leap and just have faith there's a dreamy heap of meringue down there to catch you.

filling

2 cups sliced hulled fresh strawberries

2 cups thinly sliced fresh rhubarb

1/3 cup water

1 cup sugar

2 tablespoons cornstarch

1 cup heavy cream

1 teaspoon pure vanilla extract

syrup

1/2 cup sugar

meringue

8 large egg whites, at room temperature

2 cups sugar

1. **For the filling:** Stir together the strawberries, rhubarb, and water in a medium sauce pan. Simmer gently over medium-low heat for 20 minutes, or until the berries and rhubarb are very soft. Strain the cooking liquid into a small bowl and set it aside. There should be about 1/2 cup of liquid. Crush the strawberry mixture with a potato masher or the back of a spoon and return it to the pan.

2. Whisk the sugar and cornstarch together in a small bowl and stir into the

recipe continues

strawberry mixture. Stir in the cream and bring to a simmer over low heat. Simmer for 5 minutes, or until the mixture thickens. Stir in the vanilla. Divide among six 6-ounce ramekins. Place the ramekins on a baking sheet to cool to room temperature.

3. **For the syrup:** Stir together the reserved strawberry-rhubarb cooking liquid and sugar in a small saucepan. Bring to a simmer over medium heat and cook for 5 minutes, or until the sugar dissolves and the mixture thickens slightly. Let cool to room temperature.

4. Preheat the oven to 400°F.

5. **For the meringue:** Place the egg whites in a large bowl and beat until frothy with a mixer on low speed. Increase to high speed and gradually add the sugar, beating to soft peaks. Add 3 tablespoons of the reserved strawberry-rhubarb syrup, 1 tablespoon at a time, and continuing beating to stiff peaks.

6. Spoon the meringue over the filling, spreading it to the edges of the ramekins and piling it high in the center. Bake in the upper third of the oven for 5 minutes, or until the meringue is golden brown with slightly darker peaks. Let cool to room temperature on the baking sheet, and then refrigerate 1 hour, or until chilled.

7. To serve, place each ramekin on a saucer and drizzle with the remaining strawberry-rhubarb syrup, letting it drip down the sides.

Mermaid Marshmallow Pie

MAKES ONE 9½-INCH PIE

Someone once told me this pie was "biblically good," and I do believe they were right. I invented it with my mama when I was a girl, during my "mermaid phase"; now my own daughter and I make it together. The pineapple, coconut, oranges, and nuts, like an old-time ambrosia salad, will tickle the fancy of any child, or the child inside you.

shortbread cookie pie shell

1¾ cups shortbread cookie crumbs (about 12 cookies)

6 tablespoons (¾ stick) unsalted butter, melted

filling

½ cup heavy cream, chilled

1 (8-ounce) package cream cheese, at room temperature

1 (14-ounce) can sweetened condensed milk

1 teaspoon pure vanilla extract

Pinch of salt

1 cup sweetened flaked coconut, plus 1 tablespoon for garnish

1 cup drained crushed pineapple

1 cup drained mandarin oranges

¾ cup pecan pieces

2 cups colored mini marshmallows or additional mandarin oranges, for garnish

1. **For the pie shell:** Preheat the oven to 350°F. Toss together the crumbs and butter in a medium bowl to moisten. Press the mixture onto the bottom and up the sides of a 9½-inch deep-dish pie pan. Refrigerate for at least 15 minutes to firm up the butter. Bake in the center of the oven for about 10 minutes, or until just set and fragrant. Let cool to room temperature on a wire rack.

2. **For the filling:** In a chilled medium bowl using a mixer, beat the cream on high speed until it holds firm peaks. Refrigerate until needed.

3. In a large bowl using the mixer, beat the cream cheese on medium speed until smooth. Add the condensed milk, vanilla, and salt and beat until smooth.

4. Fold in 1 cup of coconut, the pineapple, oranges, and pecan pieces. Fold in the whipped cream.

5. Pour into the pie shell and refrigerate for 4 hours, or until chilled and set. Decorate the top of the pie with the marshmallows and the remaining 1 tablespoon coconut.

Getting Out of the Mud Frozen Mud Pie

MAKES ONE 9½-INCH PIE

How do you dig yourself out of an overwhelming stack of troubles? Turns out, you don't have to do it alone.

Take an avalanche of cool, sweet ice cream. Flow it into a shell made of crushed sugar cones. Glaze it over with thick, fudgy chocolate, just enough to lock it up. Now take five spoons, get a bunch of your friends over, and eat your way out, one bite at a time, till there's a clear path to the edges and you've talked out your woes. Getting unstuck isn't easy, but it sure helps to have a few extra spoons.

sugar cone pie shell

1¾ cups ice cream sugar cone crumbs

6 tablespoons (¾ stick) unsalted butter, melted

glaze

6 ounces semisweet chocolate, chopped

1 cup confectioners' sugar

4 tablespoons (½ stick) unsalted butter

¼ cup heavy cream

2 tablespoons light corn syrup

1 teaspoon almond extract

filling

2 pints mocha almond ice cream

½ cup sliced almonds, toasted and cooled

1. **For the pie shell:** Preheat the oven to 350°F. Toss together the crumbs and butter in a medium bowl to moisten. Press the mixture onto the bottom and up the sides of a 9½-inch deep-dish pie pan. Refrigerate for at least 15 minutes to firm up the butter. Bake in the center of the oven for about 10 minutes, or until just set and fragrant. Place on a wire rack to cool to room temperature.

2. **For the glaze:** Heat the chocolate, confectioners' sugar, butter, cream, and corn syrup in a small saucepan over low heat, stirring until smooth. Remove the pan from the heat and stir in the almond

recipe continues

extract. Let sit until lukewarm. Pour half the glaze into the bottom of the pie shell and spread until even; refrigerate for 30 minutes, or until the glaze sets. Reserve the rest of the glaze.

3. **For the filling:** Let the ice cream sit at room temperature for about 10 minutes, or until soft enough to scoop and spread. Spread 2 cups of the ice cream in the pie shell.

4. If the reserved glaze has turned too firm to pour, reheat it over very low heat. Drizzle the ice cream with half the remaining glaze and sprinkle with half the almonds. Return to the refrigerator to chill for 15 minutes, then repeat the layers. Freeze for 2 hours, or until firm.

ICE CREAM PIES

The key to success with frozen pies like this one is patience. You need to make sure your ice cream is soft enough to be spreadable, then let it get cold enough to be completely firm between each layer. That means a few trips back to the refrigerator as you are assembling it and then a good long cooling-off period in the freezer before you serve it up. Skimp on time at any point in the process and you won't have distinct layers, just a soupy mess.

Thanks for Taking Me to the Moon Peanut Butter MoonPie Pie

~

MAKES ONE 9½-INCH PIE

Somebody once sent me over the moon. Well, that's a story for another day, but I can tell you that when it was time to come back down to earth, I showed him how I felt with this pie. The peanut butter cream is earthy, like a peanut butter sandwich that's been transformed into a dessert. But then the marshmallow whipped cream and the MoonPies take it straight into the stratosphere. It's a kid-friendly treat, with a little grown-up flavor in it, too. Because everyone should be free to fly to the moon once in a while.

graham cracker pie shell

1¾ cups graham cracker crumbs (about 16 sheets of crackers)

6 tablespoons (¾ stick) unsalted butter, melted

filling

1 (8-ounce) package cream cheese, at room temperature

1 cup creamy peanut butter (not all natural)

1 cup confectioners' sugar

1½ cups heavy cream, chilled

1 teaspoon pure vanilla extract

marshmallow whipped cream

1 cup heavy cream, chilled

2 tablespoons confectioners' sugar

1 cup marshmallow cream

4 Mini MoonPies, halved crosswise, for garnish

1 tablespoon grated bittersweet or semisweet chocolate, for garnish

1. **For the pie shell:** Preheat the oven to 350°F. Toss together the crumbs and butter in a medium bowl to moisten. Press the mixture onto the bottom and up the sides of a 9½-inch deep-dish pie pan. Refrigerate for at least 15 minutes to firm up the butter. Bake in the center of the oven for about 10 minutes, or until just set and fragrant. Place on a wire rack to cool to room temperature.

recipe continues

2. **For the filling:** In a medium bowl using a mixer, beat the cream cheese, peanut butter, and confectioners' sugar on medium speed until well-blended and smooth.

3. In another medium bowl, beat the cream and vanilla on high speed until it holds firm peaks. Beat the whipped cream into the cream cheese mixture on low speed. Pour the filling into the crust and smooth the top. Refrigerate for at least 3 hours, or until set.

4. **For the topping:** In a large bowl using the mixer, beat the cream and confectioners' sugar on high speed until it holds soft peaks. Add the marshmallow cream and beat to firm peaks. Scoop the topping into a pastry bag fitted with a fluted tip and pipe it decoratively over the filling.

5. Nestle the halved MoonPies into the whipped cream and sprinkle with the grated chocolate.

Index